D0606636

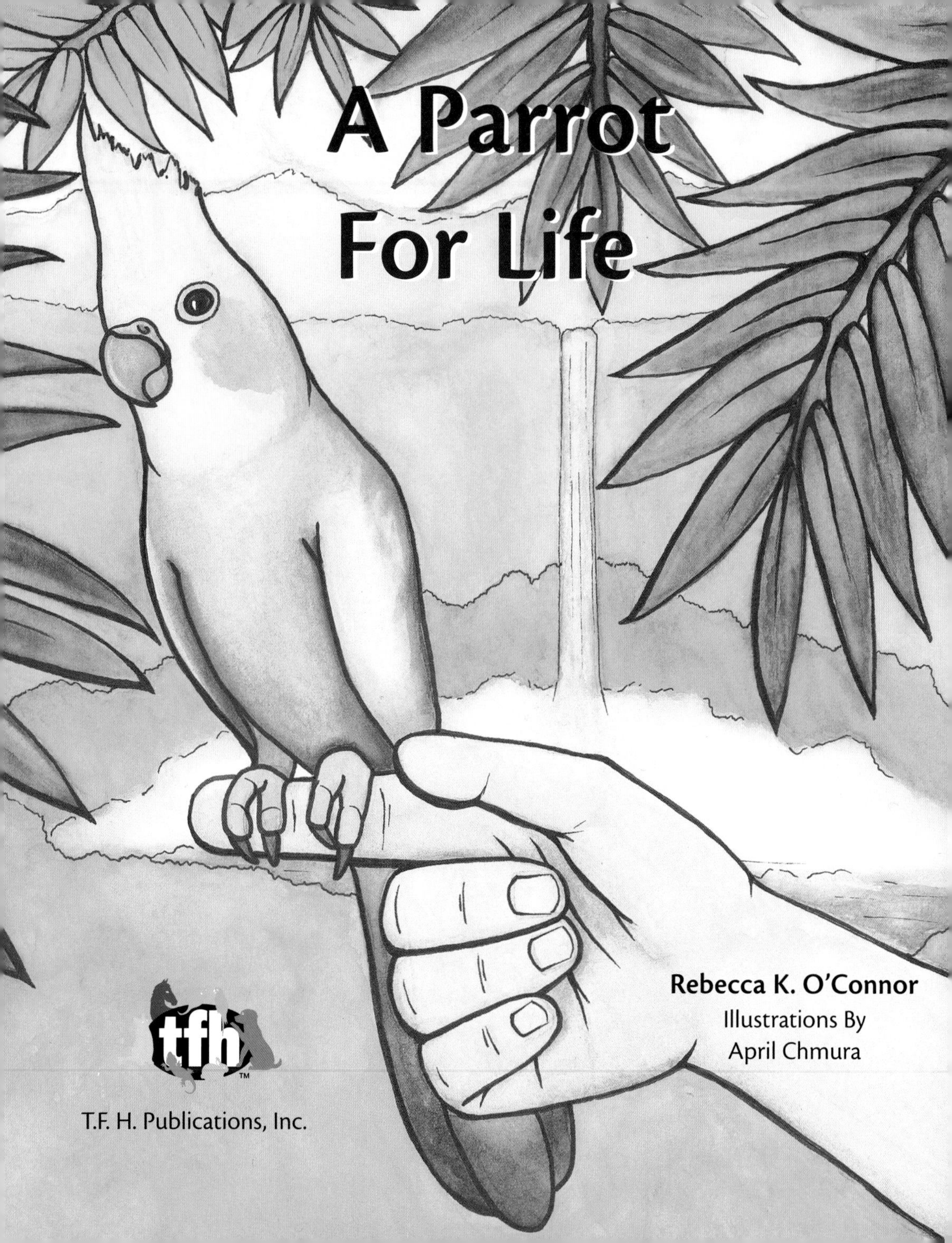

A Parrot For Life

Rebecca K. O'Connor
Illustrations By
April Chmura

tfh™
T.F. H. Publications, Inc.

A Parrot For Life

Project Team
Editor: Tom Mazorlig
Copy Editor: Stephanie Forino
Design: Mary Ann Kahn

T.F.H. Publications
President/CEO: Glen S. Axelrod
Executive Vice President: Mark E. Johnson
Publisher: Christopher T. Reggio
Production Manager: Kathy Bontz

T.F.H. Publications, Inc.
One TFH Plaza
Third and Union Avenues
Neptune City, NJ 07753

07 08 09 10 3 5 7 9 8 6 4 2

Library of Congress Cataloging-in-Publication Data
O'Connor, Rebecca.
A parrot for life : raising and training the perfect parrot companion / Rebecca O'Connor.
p. cm.
Includes index.
ISBN-13: 978-0-7938-0582-2 (alk. paper) 1. Parrots. I. Title.
SF473.P3O26 2007
636.6'865--dc22

2006024597

The Leader In Responsible Animal Care For Over 50 Years!®
www.tfh.com

Contents

Acknowledgements

It was the grandparents who raised me that nurtured my love for birds, which was surprising because birds terrified my grandmother. Much to her dismay the orphaned wild chicks I seemed to nurse and raise every spring often fledged in the house. My grandmother would pull her blouse over her face and shriek until I corralled the offending feathered demon out of the room. Yet, no one ever insisted I give up my fascination for birds.

Acknowledgements

Despite her unease, my grandmother gave me my first parrot, a lutino cockatiel for Christmas when I was ten. I was elated! It wasn't long before I managed to catch a stray gray cockatiel by leaving the lutino in a cage on the lawn to lure the lost bird. My grandparents were confounded, but merely shrugged. When no one claimed the bird, I happily had two birds.

It was my grandfather who taught me to name every bird I saw and encouraged me to love them. He once pointed out a falconer's peregrine that had lost her way and was resting on the high perch of our rooftop television antenna. He enraptured me with stories of falconry and set me down the road to being a falconer as well.

Both my grandparents left for the big blue before I found my own wings, but neither would be surprised that I eventually would be a professional bird trainer. I think they would be pleased, and I owe them a daughter's gratitude for encouraging my one true love.

I also owe those who have encouraged me on this journey. Barbara Heidenreich, a true "birds and blues" friend, has both encouraged me to leap and inspired me with leaps of her own. All of the falconers and the trainers I have worked with at NEI, Healesville Sanctuary, and The Living Desert who continue to remind me why the birds are king have my gratitude. Bobbi Brinker, whose devotion to my beloved grey parrots is beyond compare, assisted on my manuscript with words of wisdom and a proofreader's sharp eyes. Susan Friedman also deserves much thanks for her generous time and information. She is a woman truly devoted to a better world for our birds. I'm also grateful to my editor Tom Mazorlig who laughingly states he contracted the book simply on the sassy initial title, *Single... With Parrots*. And all of the animals who over the years have made me a better person by allowing me to share their world, to them I owe the very best moments of my life.

Introduction

Human beings have been fascinated with keeping parrots in their households for more than 3,000 years. The first written reference to parrots is found in the ancient *Rigveda,* written in India, where parakeets—today often referred to by their genus, *Psitticula*—were abundant and revered. It wasn't long until these feathered jewels reached countries where parrots were unknown and became treasured pets. Parrots from around the world found homes in palaces and castles. Many believe that Frederick II of Hohenstaufen, a 13th century Holy Roman Emperor, may have been the first proud owner of a sulfur-crested cockatoo in Europe. This is no surprise to anyone familiar with the monarch, who had a passion for birds, falconry in particular. Today's falconers still read Frederick's *On the Art of Hunting With Birds,* and many of them keep parrots.

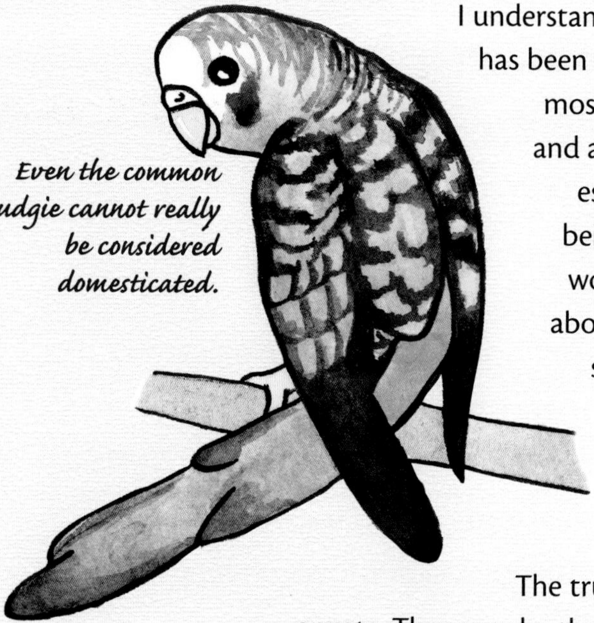

Even the common budgie cannot really be considered domesticated.

I understand Frederick's passion. My house has been home to parrots and raptors for most of my adult life, and falcons and a small flock of parrots are both essential elements to my well-being. If pressed to explain, I guess I would say that there's something about the wildness in the birds, something that keeps me enthralled and keeps me searching for ways to better communicate and connect with them.

The truth is that parrots are not dogs or cats. They may be the third most popular pet in our homes, but they are very different than most animals we keep. Dogs and cats have a long history of dependence on human beings, and in turn, a long history of humans breeding them for their best qualities. Most of our pets are domesticated and therefore well suited to living with us. And while we've been domesticating chickens, pigeons, and geese for 4,000 years, we've kept our parrots wild. In fact, only in the last few decades have many species of parrots become readily available as captive-bred pets. Most parrots, with the exception of budgies and cockatiels, are no more than a handful of generations removed from the wild.

Introduction

If you own a parrot, domestication is one of the most important concepts to understand. A handfed parrot, sweet and bonded, is only tame—not domestic. Domestication takes thousands of years. In many ways, it's a mutual arrangement. We read the body language of floppy ears, wagging canine tails, and purring felines easily because we have had a lot of practice. We also chose to breed the pets who had the most appealing characteristics, the ones who tended to sleep by the fire and allow us to stroke their fur. On the other hand, parrots are completely wild; most are only a few generations away from wild ancestors, and many of their natural behaviors can conflict with the domestic bliss that humans prefer.

Their wildness may be what I love about my parrots, but it can make them difficult pets. Parrots may scream, destroy furniture, become aggressive, and even hurt themselves. Some of them may be small, but believe me, they can have a larger presence in your home than a Great Dane. They can also be more expensive to care for than a large dog. Avian medicine is specialized and can cost far more than the care of a dog or cat. Parrots need toys, a highly varied diet, an excellent cage, a play area, and most importantly, a lot of your time. This time won't just be spent cuddling; it will also be spent cleaning, feeding, and problem solving.

Parrots don't make good pets for a single-person household because they are small and can be shut up in a cage. They aren't a better pet on a fixed income because they live on seed. If you don't have enough time to walk a dog, a parrot is not a good alternative. If you get a parrot for any of these reasons, not only are you misinformed, but both you and the parrot will be miserable.

Parrots can make good pets for single folks because they're interactive, time consuming, and rewarding. They most certainly fill your days. My house has always been lively and full of avian laughter that sounds an awful lot like my own. Parrots make my house feel like a home, but the purpose of this book is not to convince you that parrots are the perfect pet. They aren't, but if you're willing to put in the effort, they can be wonderful companions.

A relationship with a parrot is likely to last longer than a marriage.

Assuming that you've already made up your mind and you can't live without a feathered friend, this book is meant to help both of you. The time- and money-saving tips in this book are not meant to make it possible to have a parrot when you shouldn't. The tips are intended to give you more time to spend with your parrot and more money to spend on giving your friend the very best. However, some of the most important tips in this book involve behavior. Parrots can live in excess of 50 years, making this quite possibly the longest relationship of your life. The more that you learn about parrot behavior, and the more that you apply your knowledge, the better your relationship will be. A well-adjusted parrot is less destructive, less likely to scream incessantly, healthier, and happier. This will undoubtedly save you money in vet bills, evictions, and therapy for the both of you.

I applaud you for already doing your homework and reading up on how to care for your bird. Don't stop here, though! Keep reading. In the back of the book you'll find more suggestions for further research. Don't stop there, either. Professionals in avian medicine, husbandry, and behavior analysis are making huge strides in understanding how best to care for birds, and this fount of new information will continue to evolve rapidly. The possibility for a world of even happier, healthier companion parrots is quickly becoming reality. You wouldn't want to miss any of the exciting advances in our future that are sure to come.

Happy parronting!

Rebecca K. O'Connor

October 2006

Chapter 1

So You Want to Be a "Parront"?:

CHOOSING THE RIGHT PARROT

The first thing that's important to understand in choosing a parrot is that they aren't all different breeds of the same species, like the various dogs and cats are. Comparing an African grey to a green-winged macaw is like comparing a coyote and a wolf or a lion and a jaguar. They are similar animals but possess very different personality traits that assist their survival in the wild.

So You Want To Be a "Parront?"

Choosing a parrot is not as simple as picking the one who is your favorite color, although of course you'll think that the species you choose is the most beautiful of them all. The best way to choose a parrot is to do a tremendous amount of research on the behaviors of various parrots and decide which one will mesh the best with your own personality. Remember, this relationship should last longer than most marriages, so choose your parrot mate wisely!

Some Considerations

As you investigate the kaleidoscope of parrot possibilities, there are several pertinent questions you should ask yourself. What size parrot do you think you'd like? Will the beak on a green-winged macaw intimidate you? Will caring for a tiny bird like a parrotlet make you nervous? If so, maybe a medium-sized bird is just right for you. Think this through carefully. Parrots should have plenty of hands-on interaction, so you should be certain you're going to be comfortable handling your bird.

There's a big difference between a military macaw (right) and a violet-naped lory (above). Choose your parrot carefully.

Next, you need to consider how much room you have for parrot furniture, like caging and play areas. It was once thought that a big enough cage was one that allowed a parrot to open his wings. Today, parrot professionals agree that cages should be far roomier than that. Your living space will determine the size cage you can have, which will partially determine what species you can choose from. If you live in a studio apartment, a blue and gold macaw may not be the right choice for you; a smaller parrot may make more sense. You should also consider where you might be living in the future. If you're currently living in a large home but think there's a good possibility you may move somewhere less roomy in the future, take that into consideration. From now on, wherever you go, your parrot is going with you. This is a lifelong commitment. I just can't emphasize that enough.

Another consideration is noise level. How much noise are you willing to tolerate? What about your neighbors? If you live in an apartment, a high-decibel bird like any of the species of macaw or conure may call out for your eviction.

Parrots Don't Naturally Scream

I bet you're thinking "What? I just heard a parrot screaming the other day. This author is crazy!" I'm not crazy. The truth is that parrots vocalize. Some vocalizations have a propensity to be louder than others, and to some people, even the normal vocalizations of certain species can be annoying. Screaming, though, is a learned behavior. It is a frequent or even constant loud vocalization that a parrot has learned gets her something she wants, like attention or time out of the cage. Screaming isn't normal and probably isn't enjoyable for anyone, including the parrot—imagine how exhausted you would be if you had to scream at the top of your lungs for a half hour every time you wanted something. The best way to get a parrot who doesn't scream is to avoid teaching her to engage in this behavior. Take care to pay attention and reward quiet noises and behaviors that you like. It's far easier to avoid training a bird to scream than to teach her not to scream once she has learned.

Certainly, you can avoid teaching a bird to scream for what she wants, but keep in mind that parrots can have normal vocalizations that are loud. Just be sure that you and anyone within yelling distance doesn't mind the noise. If a boisterous parrot doesn't suit your home life, there are certainly quieter species you can investigate.

Lastly, how much time do you have? All parrots are going to take up a big, but rewarding, portion of your time. However, some—like lories—require a specialized diet, which will require a good deal of time to prepare. Some parrots, like cockatoos, are easily taught to enjoy as much time as possible scratching and cuddling with their owners. Others, like African greys, will be happier interacting with you in the room as opposed to occupying your hands. If you spend your nights watching television, a cockatoo tucked beneath your chin may be just the ticket to easing a stressful day. If you're a writer and spend the nights pounding away at your laptop, on the other hand, you may be happier with a grey.

Yellow-headed (above) and orange-winged (right) Amazon parrots are two frequently kept parrots.

The World of Parrots

Now that you have these all-important considerations rattling around in your head, it's time to take a look at some of the most common species of parrots available. (Keep in mind that the information provided here represents just the tip of the iceberg on a handful of species.) There are more than 300 recognized species of parrots, and every year more of those species are readily available in aviculture. In addition, each of these species has unique characteristics. When you've narrowed down your choices, be sure to talk to people who own these parrots, talk to people who swear they would never own one, and read everything you can find.

Naming common characteristics in parrots can be helpful for someone beginning an investigation into the appropriate parrot for his or her home, but sometimes these characteristics can be stereotypes. All parrot species have a propensity for the traits that are named in the following paragraphs, but none of

Talking Parrots

There are certain species that are more likely to talk, like African greys and Amazons. However, you should never count on the fact that your parrot will be a talker. Even within species, parrots are individuals. I've heard many stories of African greys who have never said a word. Mine talks up a storm, and my red-bellied parrot joins in a bit, but my 11-year-old Senegal won't speak or repeat any noises. She's very intelligent and eager to learn new tricks during training time but doesn't have the inclination to mimic sounds. I've heard other Senegals who mimic sounds and words brilliantly, but not mine. Go figure. So choose the parrot with the best personality for your home, but don't make your decision based on having a parrot who must talk. With socialization, training, and a lot of love, your parrot might just learn to talk. But even if your bird never says a word, you'll find many other reasons to love her if you choose the species that is the best fit for you.

them are a given. Each and every bird is an individual; there's still a chance that you'll get a cockatoo who doesn't want to be touched or an African grey who never speaks a word. Choosing the parrot who is right for you should be a well-informed personal decision.

Central and South American Parrots

Parrots from Central and South America are brightly colored and often noisy. The need to be heard across the rainforest has given many of these species an eardrum-busting call. If you live in an apartment, many of these birds may not be right for you. They are also parrots who travel

The 5 Worst Reasons to Get a Parrot

You should rethink your choice of having a parrot for a pet if your reason for getting one is any of the following:

1. **I don't have enough time for a dog.**
2. **I don't have enough space for a bigger pet.**
3. **I can't afford to care for a bigger pet.**
4. **Parrots are so beautiful and one would look great in my house.**
5. **Someone is giving me a parrot for free.**

Parrots need just as much time and attention as a dog needs, and these birds require plenty of room to move around. Avian medicine is specialized and expensive. Even free parrots and beautiful parrots can scream, bite, and pluck. The only good reason to get a parrot is because you cannot live without one!

and forage frequently in mixed-species groups. If you think you might be looking at having a flock down the road, you should consider choosing from the parrots from the New World. Of course, parrots playing together should always be supervised, but they might be more likely to interact if they are species that naturally travel with other species of parrots.

Amazons

There are more than 20 species of Amazon parrot. They are all medium-sized birds (10–19 inches [25 –48 cm]), mainly green with a short rounded tail. A variety of colors exists among the different species in the head, wings, and tail. Amazons can be loud, although not as loud as the macaws. Some individuals are excellent talkers, especially certain double yellow-headed, yellow-naped, and blue-fronted Amazons. Many of the Amazons I've met seem to have a real joy for singing as well as clowning around. They are also considered more likely to display aggression once they reach sexual maturity. This fast-changing temperament requires owners who are

White-bellied and black-headed caiques: avian clowns.

Two of the most popular conures are the sun conure (below) and the nanday conure (opposite)

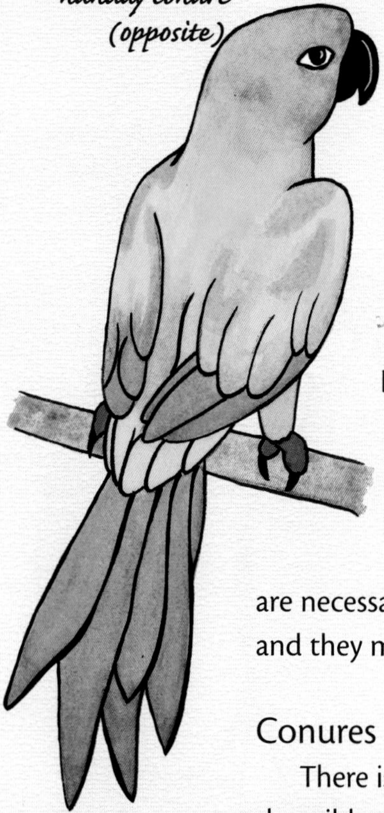

willing to become astute at reading their body language in order to prevent aggressive behavior.

Caiques

Caiques are big birds in a small parrot package, and they are a recent addition to the world of aviculture. They are friendly, outgoing birds who are festively colored and endlessly entertaining. The most commonly available species are the black-headed caique and the white-bellied caique, which are each about 9 inches (23 cm) long. They are high-energy birds in constant motion and can be very destructive if not given the appropriate means to keep their beaks busy. Their natural curiosity and intelligence can get them into trouble, so lots of toys and creative enrichment are necessary. They can be loud, but not as loud as conures, and they may also learn to talk a little.

Conures

There is a large variety of conure species that are found in the wild and that can be kept as pets. They come in a small package and feature a gorgeous array of colors. The majority of the conure species range between 7–14 inches (18–36 cm) long. Don't let their small size fool you, though; conures have big personalities and amazingly loud voices. They are not good birds in homes where they might disturb neighbors or roommates. Many conures are purchased on impulse because of their playful personalities and vibrant colors, but some buyers don't realize how loud this bird can be. This is why it's so important to be certain that a conure won't be a noise issue before you buy one. You don't want to find yourself looking for a new home for your bird in the future.

Macaws

The macaws range in size from about 24–48 inches (60–120 cm). The only thing louder than the brilliant colors of the macaw is their voice. They can certainly catch your ear with a call from across the forest, but they can also be reasonably good talkers. The most common species include the blue and gold, green-winged, scarlet, military, and hyacinth macaws. They are large birds—the hyacinth is the largest parrot at nearly 4 feet (120 cm) in length. Although macaws can be loud and domineering, they can also be good-natured and loving. Their beauty and charming personalities sometimes make them the victim of impulse buyers, so be sure to think carefully before you buy one. Macaws can make wonderful pets, but they can be more than a handful.

Mini-Macaws

With all the will and half the size of their larger cousins, mini-macaws can be the right parrot for someone who loves the "macaw personality" but who doesn't have the space for the full-sized parrot. Some of the most common species are the severe, yellow-collared, and Hahn's macaws. These birds range from 12–20 inches (30–51 cm) in length, a more manageable size than the full-sized macaws. They have all the curiosity and playfulness of the larger macaws but at a lower volume. They still can't be considered quiet parrots, but they cannot match the lung capacity of their larger cousins. Mini-macaws can be excellent talkers and incredible clowns.

White-capped pionus are often quieter than conures and Amazons.

Pionus

There are five different species of pionus parrots that are commonly kept as pets. They are all about 10–12 inches (25–30 cm) long, feature a similar body shape, and have red feathers under their tails. They come in a variety of colors, and in the sunlight, you can see the amazing complexity and shading of their feathers. They can be rather sensitive birds when compared to conures or macaws; in fact, they tend to be shyer and more reserved. If you are looking for a more boisterous and clownish bird, then pionus parrots may not be right for you. They can, however, make great pets for those who are looking for a quieter, gentler bird—but remember, there's no such thing as a silent parrot. Pionus parrots have limited talking ability, but they may learn a few words and a lot of fun sounds.

Quaker (Monk) Parakeets

There are many owners who swear that Quakers are the best possible parrots. However, in many states, this bird is illegal. Escaped parrots have established feral flocks in many cities in the United States, especially in Florida. Fearing that the parrots may displace native wildlife or harm crops, they

One Parrot or Two?

Parrot owners in a single-person household often ask if they should get two parrots instead of one. This way, perhaps the parrots can keep each other company during the day. Two bonded parrots of the same species sharing a cage will certainly keep each other company. However, they will likely prefer each other to you. If you're looking for a companion parrot, a solitary parrot is almost always best. However, there's no arguing that parrots in separate cages are probably enriched by sharing a room. My small group of African parrots functions like a flock. They are always eating, preening, and napping at the same time. I imagine that although they don't enjoy each other's company enough to play together, they must naturally get comfort from being a part of a flock. However, I've also met many well-adjusted parrots from single-parrot homes. If you care for more than one parrot, you will spend more time in their care and cleaning, and your one-on-one time will be split between the parrots in your home. If you work a nine-to-five job, you will need to decide whether your pet will benefit more from a multiple-parrot household or from your undivided attention.

are banned in California, Hawaii, Kentucky, Tennessee, Wyoming, Pennsylvania, and Rhode Island. Laws change, so be sure to check before you buy a Quaker parrot, even if you don't live in one of these states. These predominantly green parrots are only about 11 inches (28 cm) long but have large personalities. Some individuals are notably excellent talkers, and in fact, they can be noisy, although not as noisy as conures and macaws. They are playful, curious, intelligent, and can also be extremely territorial. However, if socialized properly, Quaker parrots can make excellent pets.

African grey parrots are intelligent and sensitive birds.

African Parrots

African parrots are considered quieter than many species of parrots. All of these species are capable of a great deal of noise, but African parrots tend to keep their noise level in the lower decibel range. For example, my flock, consisting of a grey, a Senegal, and a red-bellied, cannot be heard on the street when the doors and windows of my house are closed. However, when outside my home, I can hear the blue and gold macaw that lives the next block over. Another aspect of the African parrots to consider is that they live in single species groups. This means that you can't expect them to get along well with other species once they've reached maturity.

African Greys

The African grey is a medium-sized gray parrot with a white facial patch and a red tail. There are two subspecies: the larger, more silver-colored Congo and the smaller, slate-gray Timneh. The Timneh has a bone-colored upper beak instead of the black one that the Congo features, and the Timneh has a darker tail. Greys are considered fantastic talkers and can match their owners' voices perfectly, as well as myriad other household sounds. A grey who has learned to imitate the smoke alarm can be maddeningly loud, but these birds mostly are considered one of the quieter species. They are also thought to be very smart. Intelligent and wary birds who normally ground feed, greys can be more sensitive to their environment than other species. In fact, they are sometimes referred to as neurotic. Although some individuals enjoy constant cuddling, most greys are rather

The Five Most Important Things to Ask When Buying a Parrot

If you're going to buy or rescue a parrot, the more questions you ask, the better. However, if it's love at first sight and you are tripping over your tongue, at least try to remember to ask these five questions:

1. What is this parrot's history?
2. What do you feed her?
3. What's her personality like?
4. Does she have any behavior problems?
5. Has she been to the vet recently for a checkup?

aloof. However, their personality has found a huge, loyal fan club.

Lovebirds

Lovebirds make excellent pets for first-time parrot keepers. They are tiny (5–6 inches [13–15 cm]) and come in a wonderful array of color mutations. The most common species are peach-faced, Fischer's, and masked. Generally, they do not talk but are highly playful and affectionate. However, to have an interactive lovebird, you need to acquire her at a young age and work with her frequently. The introduction of another lovebird will spell the end of human bonding. As the name implies, lovebirds easily and deeply bond with their avian mate. Their lifespan is only 5 to 12 years, so they are less of a commitment than a larger parrot, but they lack the range of vocalizations and deeper interactions that are possible with some of the larger parrots.

Lovebirds form intense bonds with each other or their parronts.

Poicephalus

Poicephalus parrots, named for their genus, include the red-bellied parrot, Senegal parrot, Meyer's parrot, and Jardine's parrot. They are small birds, ranging in size from

8–12 inches (20–30 cm), and are mainly green with other splashes of color on the chest, rump, and head. Many owners consider them to be perfect apartment birds, with a smaller voice to match their stature. They can talk, though often not as clearly as birds who are considered good talkers. They are also highly intelligent, extremely trainable, and good-natured if properly socialized.

Psittacula

Psittacula is a genus of parrot that is also referred to as the ring-necked parakeets. The genus includes more than a dozen species of Afro-Asian parrots. All of them are sleek and regal in stature, with long tails and pastel colors. The Indian ring-necked parakeet is one of the most common of the genus. She measures about 16 inches (41 cm) long and has a history as a companion parrot since Roman times. The psittaculas were and still are highly prized pets because of their ability to talk. Although their speech isn't as clear as larger parrots, their vocabulary can be tremendous—some

The Senegal (left) and Jardine's parrots (above) are two species of Poicephalus.

say up to 250 words. They can be somewhat loud and territorial and so require constant contact and work to remain tame. Solitary birds tend to make better pets because a pair will bond together and not be as responsive to people. With enough attention, though, these parrots can be playful and sweet companions.

Australasian Parrots

Australasian parrots are a diverse group. Some of the species are completely unique, just like so many of the animals found in Australia. Like the New World parrots, many of the Australasian parrots are found in the rain forest and can have big voices. The group boasts one of the most popular groups of parrots, the cockatoos. It also comprises two of the best parrots for first-time parrot owners: budgies and cockatiels.

Cockatiels are bred in many colors, including the normal gray (above) and lutino varieties (opposite).

Budgerigars (Budgies)

Often called parakeets, budgerigars are hands down the most popular pet bird. Show budgies, frequently called English budgies, are about 9–10 inches (23–25 cm) long, and American budgies, those normally seen in pet shops, are smaller. Although their natural color is a deep green, they have been bred for 250 different color mutations. They can be affectionate, playful, and trainable. Some individuals can be astoundingly excellent talkers, as well. Although they have a tiny voice that isn't as clear as a large parrot's, budgerigars can learn to say hundreds of words. Happy budgies chatter a great deal, but they are not loud birds and can be a good choice for apartment dwellers. They are small and easy to care for, with less significant living areas to clean. However, they do have a very short life span of generally 5 to 7 years, although with proper care, some live as long as 13 years.

Cockatiels

Cockatiels are small parrots about 14–15 inches (36–38 cm) in length, with a long tail and a jaunty little head crest. They have been bred for a wide range of color variations but are normally predominantly gray. Cockatiels are charming birds with huge personalities. Males can learn to say a few words, and both sexes can be wonderful whistlers. They are quieter parrots, so they can make good apartment birds. Many people will tell you that cockatiels make a good first parrot because they are small and easily managed. However, this is not a good reason to get a cockatiel. You should only make a cockatiel your choice if this bird is truly your first choice. They cannot talk as well as some of the larger parrots and may not have other traits that owners find desirable in the larger birds. It would be unfair to buy a cockatiel as a "starter bird" to only later have the parrot ignored in favor of a larger, more desirable pet.

Cockatoos

Cockatoos certainly have an army of fans. These birds range in size from medium to large (12– 26 inches [30–66 cm]). The most common species are mainly white with a magnificent crest that is splashed with color. The commonly kept species are Goffin's, Moluccan, umbrella, citron, sulfur-crested, and lesser sulfur-crested. However, there are many others. All share a love of adoration and cuddling, making them hands-on parrots. One drawback to these affectionate birds is that they shed a tremendous amount of dust, so they may not be a good fit for people with allergies. These birds are also known for their ability to chew. Sulfur-crested cockatoos in Australia travel in great flocks that can cause tremendous destruction to crops. Their job in the wild is to forage through the eucalyptus, finding food and spreading seeds. Flocks of these busy-beaks can also inflict tremendous damage on phone lines and other interesting chew toys. So it should be no surprise that a cockatoo is capable of decimating your living room furniture.

Sulfur-crested cockatoos frequently love to cuddle.

Eclectus

Male and female eclectus were thought to be two different species until biologists realized that the bright-green birds are the males and the brilliant red birds are the females. Parrots in the genus *Eclectus* are about 12–14 inches (30–36 cm) long, and their unique feathering looks a little like hair. These birds are clever and playful, and if properly socialized, can be excellent talkers and mimics. They are generally quiet and more subdued compared to other parrots. They require a little extra sensitivity from their owners and don't bond as strongly as some other species of parrots. If you are hoping for the strong tactile bond of a bird like a cockatoo, the more aloof eclectus may not be for you. They do produce far less dust than cockatoos and most other parrots, which may be a consideration if you have allergies.

Male (below) and female (left) eclectus differ greatly in color.

Lories and Lorikeets

Lories and lorikeets are brush-tongued parrots who mainly feed on nectar and pollen in the wild. Lories are larger, heavier-bodied birds with squared-off tails. Lorikeets are more slender and have longer, tapering tails. Both types are gorgeous birds with glossy feathers that come in a rainbow of hues. These parrots range in size between 7–15 inches (18–38 cm). They are complete clowns and excellent talkers, although their voices aren't very clear. Outgoing and charming, many lory lovers feel they are the perfect pet. Much controversy still exists regarding the best diet for lories and lorikeets, which in the past owners had to create on their own. Today, liquid nectar mix and dry mixes are available. However, an owner should plan to supply ample fresh fruit, vegetables, and greens for their bird. Lories tend to have looser droppings than other parrots due to the amount of liquid in their diet, making cleaning up after them more difficult.

Rainbow lories and other lories eat mostly nectar, pollen, and fruit in nature.

A Word About Cost

You'll notice that there has been no mention of the going price of the more common parrots I've discussed. When all is said and done, the majority of your costs are not going to come from the purchase of the parrot herself. No matter the size of the bird, a lifetime of vet bills, toys, and caging costs are going to be fairly similar. (Of course, a budgie can be a "budget bird" compared to a green-winged macaw, but among the larger parrots, the cost is similar.) With this in mind, don't make your choice of parrot based on the cost of the bird.

There are many other reasons why a parrot's price tag shouldn't be the decision maker.

In some states, you can still buy unweaned parrots, who often come with a smaller price tag than a fully grown parrot. This means that the bird still needs to be hand-fed because she is too young to feed herself. Hand-feeding is time consuming, and most responsible breeders will not sell their parrots unweaned. Many things can go wrong during hand-

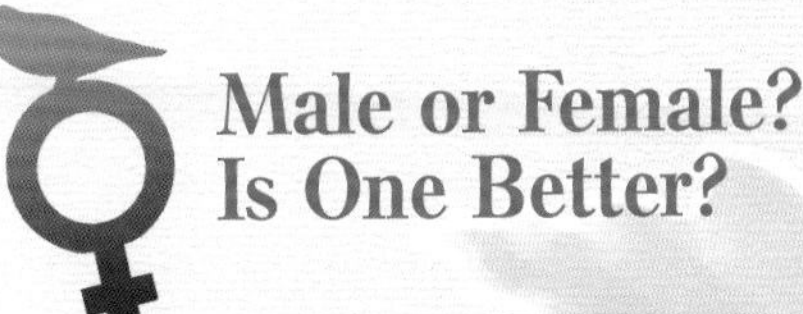

Male or Female? Is One Better?

In most parrot species, it is difficult to distinguish males from females. There are a few species that are obviously sexually dimorphic, like the *Eclectus* and *Psittacula* parrots, but most look nearly identical. Of course, the parrots can tell the difference perfectly well, but even experienced breeders can't always differentiate between the sexes. Today, it is easy to discover the sex of your bird with certainty. You can have your bird sexed through DNA examination at any visit to the veterinarian. Your vet will send a blood sample out for a definitive answer and get the results back to you generally within a few weeks. Knowing your bird's sex is important if you want to breed the bird or are uncertain whether to name your new friend George or Georgia. It can also help in the diagnosis of illness. If you are certain of your bird's sex, your vet may save valuable time ruling out sex-related medical conditions, such as egg binding if your bird is a male. However, either of the sexes of most species can be good companions, with the exception of possibly cockatoos, in which males can exhibit extreme aggression as adults. If well socialized and given plenty of attention and care, most parrots—boys and girls—can be wonderful pets.

feeding, especially when the bird is weaning (switching over to feeding herself). This is a tricky time for keeping the parrot healthy and encouraging socialization. Any missteps could negatively affect the bird for the rest of her life. The money saved isn't worth the risk of heartache you might have down the road.

Don't let cost be a factor if you have your heart set on one of the more commonly available species, either. If you really want an African grey parrot, but a Senegal only costs half as

Where to Buy Your Parrot

You may feel sorry for that "parrot in the window" at the pet shop, but buying a parrot on impulse is never wise. Do your research, and find out exactly how well the pet shop manages its birds. You need to know how well that bird was socialized, what bad behaviors she may have learned, and even how old she is. Make sure pet shop employees are parrot savvy, or they won't be able to help you with questions about the bird after you've purchased her. The other issue is the health of the bird. In order to avoid being separated from the flock in the wild, parrots are adept at hiding their illnesses until it is too late to help them. Because of this trait, make sure the birds at the shop are tested for illnesses and are looked after by a capable vet. This is also true of buying a parrot at a bird mart.

If you can't find a pet store that is up to par, sometimes the best place to go is to a local breeder. Again, talk to as many breeders as you can find in your area, and ask a lot of questions. See if you can visit their facilities or at least talk to them about their breeding practices, how they socialize their babies, what sort of diet they feed, and how their birds are housed. A good breeder will not only provide you with a well-adjusted parrot to begin with, but she can also be a continuous source of advice and knowledge throughout your relationship with your parrot.

much, don't buy the Senegal parrot just because she costs less. Trust me. I did this and ended up buying a grey six months after I purchased my first parrot anyway. More than a decade later, I still adore them both, but everyone wondered why I didn't just buy a grey in the first place. Buying a "second choice" won't save you money. Be patient and buy your first choice when you are totally prepared.

If you find your favorite flavor of parrot "on sale," you should ask questions. If she is an adult, she may come with a multitude of problems that aren't obvious, or worse, she could have been smuggled into the country. And don't ever deceive yourself into believing that there is such a thing as a "free parrot." Think long and hard before taking a parrot from a friend. Consider this a marriage; this is 'til death do you part. Would you immediately marry your friend's ex if she offered him to you?

Rescue Me!

Rescuing an unwanted parrot can be a very fulfilling option but not if you don't know what you're getting into. If you are thinking of rescuing a parrot, make sure to use your head as well as your heart. Raising a well-mannered parrot is a difficult enough prospect; a parrot with a history can be a frustrating puzzle of bad behaviors in a beautiful feathered package. Not knowing how these behaviors evolved can make fixing them a daunting task, especially for someone inexperienced in parrot behavior. If your heart is so big that you are sure you are up to the task of adopting a troubled bird, be prepared.

It isn't true that only young parrots can bond to someone. Parrots who have been re-homed again and again generally are willing to bond with the next kind heart. After all, being a parrot in the wild is risky business. Wild parrots frequently lose mates and later bond with new ones. If you choose to bring a rescue parrot or an older parrot into your home, it certainly isn't a hopeless endeavor. The new parrot could make a fantastic pet—just make sure you are willing and able to deal with already established problem behaviors.

If it's possible, find out as much information and background as you can about the parrot you are considering. If she came from a home that could no longer care for her, see if you can talk to the prior owners. If she's coming to you from a foster home where she has lived in the interim, be sure to take the foster parents out to dinner and quiz them mercilessly. All the little things can make a big difference in building a relationship with a difficult bird. For example, knowing her favorite food can help to win her friendship. Knowing her fears can help you avoid negative experiences or accidentally set back progress in building a relationship. Thus, if you know the parrot is terrified of vacuums, you'll be able to introduce the vacuum slowly and not give her a meltdown on her first day in a new home.

If you think it's possible that you might need some extra help, seek out a good behavior consultant in your area. Be sure to find someone before bringing your rescue parrot home. Check with your local pet stores, bird clubs, bird supply stores, and veterinarians to see if they can recommend anyone. A good avian behavior consultant, well versed in positive reinforcement training techniques, will have plenty of experience to help guide you in creating a wonderful relationship with your parrot.

In the next chapter, we'll look at the many other aspects that should be considered before your new housemate comes home.

No Free Parrots

You may sometimes see an advertisement for a free parrot in a newspaper or have an acquaintance offer to give you a parrot. Just remember that even if the bird herself is free, there are always other costs. These include vet visits, new toys, food, a new cage, and more. Also, there are other less obvious costs. If the free parrot has behavior problems, it will cost you time and energy (and maybe consultant's fees) to correct these problems. Think carefully before taking on a "free" parrot.

Chapter 2

Creating a Parrot Paradise:

SEETTING UP SPACE

Setting up your home for your new parrot is crucial. Proper housing and play areas can make all the difference in the well-being of your bird. In addition, thoughtfully setting up your home to care for a parrot means that you can arrange her housing to allow for easy cleanup, as well as incorporate time- and money-saving strategies.

Cage Choices

A well-constructed cage can cost as much or more than your parrot. This fact prompts many new parrot owners to try to find other ways to save money. Don't scrimp on your parrot's cage, though. (Fear not—we'll be discussing many other ways to save money on things that you will purchase for the rest of your parrot's life.) Hopefully, your newly beloved bird will be spending a lot of time outside of it, but it is still your bird's home. If you choose well, you only have to buy your parrot a cage once. So spend as much money as needed to get the biggest and best cage possible.

You should find a cage that is made of high-quality materials like stainless steel or powder-coated wrought iron. These cages are nontoxic and more durable than most other types. Plastic cages with thin wiring are not the best choice for long-term housing. Remember, too, that if you get a large cage, it will be a prominent piece of your household décor for a long time. You may as well get a cage that both you and your parrot will enjoy.

A Used Cage Is not a Bargain

Try not to buy a used cage. If the cage is in excellent shape and was obviously crafted in the last ten years, it might work fine for your bird. Just be sure to disinfect it. However, older cages may have been crafted with lead and zinc, which are both toxic to birds. Flaking paint, galvanized wire, and exposed solder can be toxic to your new friend. Ideally, purchase a shiny new cage that is unquestionably safe.

Your bird's cage should be as large as possible. Generally speaking, you can't get too big of a cage. You do, however, need to be mindful of the cage bar spacing. The smallest birds, like lovebirds, budgies, and cockatiels, should be in cages that have bars spaced 1/2 inch (1.3 cm) apart. Parrots the size of conures, poicephalus, caiques, and pionus should have bars spaced no wider than 3/4 inch (1.9 cm) apart. For medium-sized parrots like African greys and Amazons, the bars should be spaced no wider than 1 inch (2.5 cm) apart. Large macaws and cockatoos can have bars spaced as wide as 1.5 inches (3.8 cm) apart. Bar spacing is critical to your bird's safety; inappropriate spacing could allow the parrot to get her head caught between the bars, which could be fatal.

If you lived in a cage, you'd want it to be as large as possible; your parrot is no different.

Square and rectangular cages make better choices than round cages because they allow for more climbing room, especially if they have a dome-shaped top. Make sure that there are horizontal bars allowing for an easier climb. The other problem with rounded cages is that they have bars with spacing that decreases near the top, a place where a playing parrot can get her toes caught. Your best bet is a standard boxy cage.

Zinc Poisoning

Zinc poisoning has become a more frequent diagnosis in pet parrots. Some disagreement exists within the veterinary community regarding how much of a problem this truly is, but as a parrot owner, keep on the safe side and try to keep zinc out of your bird's environment. Zinc is a common metal used in coating iron and steel to prevent rust. Anything that is galvanized contains zinc. Birds who chew metal parts are likely to become poisoned from continued exposure to this metal. If your bird doesn't chew on metal, you probably have little to worry about. However, if she does, try to make sure all accessible metal is stainless steel or powder coated. If you are uncertain about metal quick links and other toy parts, check with the company that produces your toys and play gyms, and make sure that they are zinc free.

You will quickly discover that parrot cages fitting these specifications are numerous, so choose one that will work well for your household. Look for cages with pull-out trays for easy cleaning. Cages with grates will keep your parrot from walking through the mess that accumulates at the bottom. Access doors to food bowls are incredibly convenient, allowing bowls to be changed without opening the main cage door. Keep in mind that someone will have to watch your parrot if you ever go on a trip, and access doors will make things especially easy for your pet-sitter. Make sure, too, that you choose a cage with doors that can be foolproofed against a clever parrot who might learn to let herself out. Also, look for anything on the cage that might become a hazard. Scrollwork and other intricate designs on a cage are not appropriate for an acrobatic parrot who might get her toes caught.

Once you've found the perfect cage, be sure to think carefully about the perfect place to put it. A parrot's cage should be kept in a place where the temperature is comfortable for her. The dwelling also should not be positioned in direct sunlight, where a bird might overheat. Your parrot will probably be happier in a high-traffic area where she can interact with you as frequently as possible, rather than a back bedroom. However, the parrot should not live in the kitchen, where her delicate respiratory system can be affected by cooking and cleaning fumes.

Natural branches make the best parrot perches.

Perching

Now that you have your cage and a place to set it up, consider the perching inside of it. Birds can't sit like people or lay down like dogs and cats. In the wild, they would spend much time on the wing; in our homes, though, they are almost always on their feet. You should give your bird's feet special attention. An injured foot on a constantly standing parrot can be very difficult to heal, so it is important that a parrot's perching be appropriate and varied.

The perches in your parrot's cage should be of a large enough diameter that she can't reach her feet all the way around the perch. Improperly sized branches can cause arthritis and muscle atrophy. Perches should also vary in size, because a variety of perching sizes will allow your parrot to exercise the muscles in her feet. You can also find perches made of various materials.

Natural branches make the best perches. Look for branches that are pesticide free and that come from nontoxic trees such as apple, crab apple, ash, birch, cottonwood, elm, fir, mulberry, pine, and willow. Manzanita is another readily available type of wood, but it is a hard and slippery wood that, if used, should be roughed or grooved to add traction. Many parrots will quickly destroy natural perches that are made of soft wood like pine, but this is fun for them. Not only do they have perching, but they also have a great toy. You can cut branches from your own trees, leaving the bark on for extra fun, while saving money and resting assured that the branches are free of pesticides. These branches can be easily secured to the cage with a long screw and a washer or lag studs, washers, and wing nuts. Just be sure that the perch sits solidly after installation and does not wobble, or your parrot will not feel secure sitting on it.

Top Five Dangers Inside the Cage

5

1. Zinc poisoning
2. Frayed rope toys
3. Choking
4. Toxic fumes (from air fresheners, scented candles, Teflon, etc.)
5. Poisoning (feeding poisonous or moldy food)

Other perching materials include plastic and cement. Plastic perches are often slippery, but they can be sanded to make them easier for the parrot to manage. Cement perches can be too rough for extensive perching but are excellent for keeping toenails rounded. Seashell perches are another good alternative. When using rougher perches, check your parrot's feet frequently for red spots, and make sure they aren't placed in the highest location in the cage, which may make them the most frequently used perches. Your parrot should have several perches in the cage at various heights, but don't overcrowd. Be sure there's some wing room as well.

Poisonous Plants List

One place to check if a plant is poisonous or not is at the University of California, Davis. The URL for this site is http://envhort.ucdavis.edu/ce/king. Another site to check is the ASPCA poisonous plants list at http://www.aspca.org/site/PageServe r?pagename=pro_apcc_toxicplants.

Playing Outside the Cage

Play gyms and parrot trees are important additions to the perfect parrot home, because they allow a bird to spend time outside the cage and interact with her human family. In fact, your bird should enjoy as much supervised time out of the cage as possible. Before you start letting your parrot wander freely on a gym, though, be certain that your home is bird-proofed.

Gyms are generally a combination of branches designed to encourage a bird to explore and climb. Tabletop gyms may be moved from room to room for convenience, but they are often small enough that a parrot might quickly find interest elsewhere. The larger gyms are upright branches measuring approximately 5 feet (1.5 m) tall. The branches are secured to a stand that is designed to make it more difficult for a parrot to climb down. This type of gym also contains myriad options for hanging toys.

Many cages come with cagetop perches for a play area, which can also be a great option for time out of the cage. Remember, though, that gyms can be placed in rooms other than where the parrot cage resides, such as the home office or in any other room that you frequent.

Parrot-Proofing

Before you bring your parrot home, look around and remove all household dangers. Many seemingly innocuous household items pose a serious threat to pet birds.

Teflon-coated pans are one of the biggest dangers to companion parrots.

The first and probably most dangerous item is nonstick cookware. If you own anything with a Teflon coating, get rid of it. It isn't worth the risk. Under normal conditions, the cookware is perfectly safe, but if heated above 530°F (277°C), the coating becomes unstable and emits acidic fumes. You may think this won't occur, but it has happened to many vigilant parrot owners. All you have to do is put a pan on the stove with the burner on and accidentally forget it. Perhaps the phone will ring or someone will come to the door, and you'll become distracted. The fumes won't hurt you, but they will cause your bird to gasp for air, and she will die almost instantly. Your bird doesn't even have to be in the same room as the cookware. To be safe, give away any cookware that contains nonstick coating, and inspect other heated items for Teflon. Even some space heaters have Teflon coating and have been implicated in pet parrot deaths. In addition, never have a self-cleaning oven set on "clean" if you have birds in the house, because this will cause the emission of Teflon fumes.

Your bird is going to spend time out of the cage, so remove potential hazards from around his cage or play area. Don't take this to mean that it's a good idea to let your bird roam freely. No bird should

Common Toxic Household Plants

Check all plants for toxicity before placing them in the beak zone. Here's a short list of some of the most common poisonous plants to help you recognize the potential dangers.

- Azalea
- Castor Bean
- Cyclamen
- Dieffenbachia
- Kalanchoe
- Lily
- Oleander
- Poinsettia
- Rhododendron
- Sago Palm
- Tulip/Narcissus/Daffodil/Hyacinth (bulbs)
- Yew

Parrot proofing includes covering up electrical cords.

ever be left unsupervised, especially one who is clipped and unable to get herself out of danger. Free-roaming clipped parrots get stepped on and are often badly injured or killed. However, they will try to free-range and will certainly get into any trouble within their reach. Your job is to figure out what that trouble might be and head it off in advance.

The first things to remove from the bird area are potentially poisonous plants. There are many reputable sites on the Internet that list safe and unsafe house plants. Most university horticulture departments have such a list and will probably have it posted on the department's website. Most avian vets also have a list in their office. Many safe houseplants exist, so remove potentially toxic plants from your home. It only takes a minute for a parrot to shred a plant and ingest a toxic mouthful. Remember this when well-meaning suitors bring you a gift of plants. Poinsettia is beautiful at Christmas, but it's also incredibly toxic.

Also, check for any other potential dangers, such as things that parrots can climb into, knock over, or get tangled in. Use your imagination—your parrot certainly will! Open toilets are a place where many a parrot has drowned or aspirated bacteria-filled water. Electrical cords and outlets should also be childproofed. More than a decade ago, I heard a loud snap and sizzling noise. I ran into the parrot room and found my Senegal smacking her beak, having severed the light cord in front of her. My Senegal was fine, but you can bet every cord in my house is tucked away, safe from parrot beaks. Be aware of dangers for flying parrots, such as open toilets, ceiling fans, and pots of boiling liquids. Even clipped parrots can get into trouble or get stepped on.

Now that you have some idea how to keep your parrot's area safe, you should also give some thought to keeping it clean.

Keeping It Clean

If you want to keep a fresh house and a healthy parrot, you're going to be doing a lot of cleaning. Parrot cages need light cleaning daily and a serious scrubbing every three months or so. You are also going to have to clean the floors

Top Five Dangers in the House

1. Teflon-coated appliances and cookware
2. Ceiling fans
3. Pots and pans cooking on the stove
4. Open doors
5. Other pets

Parrots are messy; be prepared to clean up your bird's area frequently.

and the walls anywhere near your bird's cage. If you are renting, take special care to avoid chewed walls and permanent carpet stains. Remember, your next landlord will check up on you by speaking with your previous landlord. You wouldn't want your parrot to make it expensive or impossible to rent another place.

Around the Cage

There are several ways to save the carpet beneath your parrot's cage. If the cage sits on linoleum or tile, your job will be easier, but most people have to deal with carpeting. One of the easiest ways to save the carpet is to purchase remnants. Carpet remnants are inexpensive and can be placed beneath and around the cage, then discarded and replaced when overly stained. Another great trick is to purchase attractive sheets of linoleum or vinyl tiles. These can be glued to a large piece of painted plywood and placed beneath the cage. It will be easier to roll the cage and clean beneath it, not to mention the carpet will be preserved. Plastic office chair mats also make great carpet protectors. Sheets of plastic work as well but aren't nearly as attractive and easy to clean.

Be careful where you place your cage. You'll be amazed at how far a parrot can fling her soft food. You'll also be surprised at what she can reach to chew. If you own a house, you may want to paint the walls with a high-quality high-gloss acrylic paint that easily wipes clean. The cheaper paint normally used in an apartment will wear away with your scrubbing, but a piece of paneling or acrylic placed behind the cage can save the paint job.

Baking soda is a great parrot-safe cleanser.

In the Cage

Just like your mother told you, periodic cleaning will save you time in serious scrubbing down the road. More than that, a daily routine of cleaning the cage with hot soapy water and regularly disinfecting it can protect your bird from many health issues.

The best substrate for the floor of your parrot's cage is newspaper. Corncob and other litters can harbor bacteria and be flung about. Newspaper is nontoxic, inexpensive, and easy to roll up and discard on a daily basis.

Food and water bowls should be scrubbed daily; the water bowls of "soup-making" birds (birds that defecate or drag food into the water bowl) need more frequent cleaning. An extra set or two of bowls can save you time; put the dirty bowls in the dishwasher and exchange them with those that are already clean. You should also disinfect bowls on a weekly basis. There are several options these days for disinfecting. Veterinarians most commonly recommend bleach. Empty cages should be taken outside, scrubbed with hot soapy

Grapefruit Seed Extract

Grapefruit seed extract (GSE) is a relatively new disinfectant that is readily available in most health food stores. It is said to be an effective antiviral, antibacterial, antifungal, and antiseptic agent. It is nontoxic and can be used to clean surfaces around the house, as well as to clean fruits and vegetables. There are even claims that GSE can cure some diseases. Many breeders and vets highly recommend its use.

water, and disinfected every three months or so, depending on how dirty they get. Once scrubbed, spray the cage down with a bleach solution of 4 ounces of bleach per gallon of water (118 ml per 3.8 l), and let the cage dry in the sun. Afterward, hose it off with fresh water. Make sure your bird is in a safe place while his cage is being cleaned.

There are several other products on the market that can assist in easy cleaning and disinfecting. Pet Focus, Canopy Quick Clean, Doodle, and Poop Off are a few of the avian-safe cleansers that are readily available, and more products are developed every year. Check with your local breeder and veterinarian to see what they recommend for cleaning and disinfecting.

Household Cleaners

As you clean the rest of your house, keep in mind that many cleansers and cleaning products are toxic to birds. These animals have extremely sensitive respiratory systems and can be affected by fumes and aerosols. Any cleansers that have strong fumes, like oven cleaners and pine-scented products, should not be used around your parrot. The rule of thumb is that if it smells strong to you, it is likely too strong for your parrot.

A simmering pan of ginger, cloves, and cinnamon will cover any bird-related odors.

There are still safe cleansers out there that you can use in normal household applications. Look carefully at the labels, and smell the product before you buy it. Don't overlook cleaning with old-fashioned home tricks, either. Baking soda is still a wonderful and safe cleanser. In fact, a paste of baking soda and water can clean just about anything with a little elbow grease—even your oven. It can also remove odors and grease stains in your carpet. A mixture of vegetable-based liquid soap and water in a spray bottle is an excellent cleanser for just about anything. Linoleum floors can be cleaned with 1/2 cup (118 ml) of white vinegar mixed with 1 gallon (3.8 l) of hot water. Try to use safer methods to clean—you'll be helping out the environment as well as your parrot.

Common Scents

Other products that are meant to make your house smell fresh and wonderful can be toxic to your bird. Aerosol air fresheners are dangerous. Carpet fresheners should be avoided, as well as scented oils and incense. Recently, several parrot deaths have been attributed to scented candles. Avoid having any heavily perfumed products in your house. In general, burning anything releases irritating particles into the air, so take this into consideration where your parrot is concerned.

Quit Bugging: Keeping Insects out of the Cage

If you have parrots and live in a temperate climate, chances are you're going to have insects in your cage eventually. If you live in an apartment, insect invasions can be especially problematic. Your apartment may be spotless, but if your neighbors live in a pigsty, the insects they're collecting are sure to come visit you. Spraying pesticides is not an option, but there are a few nontoxic ways to deal with ants and roaches. (And remember—the best way to deal with insect infestations is, of course, to keep your cage as clean as possible.)

If ants are lining up to eat out of your parrot's bowls, try rubbing some oil around the legs of the cage. Any oil will work, but I usually use olive oil because it's thick and seems to last a long time. The ants will not cross an oily substance, and if all roads are blocked to the food dish, your problem is solved. If the oil isn't doing the trick, put the legs of the cage in small dishes of water. Crocks, plastic storage containers, or anything similar will work as long as you keep water in them. The ants won't swim to get to the cage.

If you have a roach problem, check to be sure that there is nowhere in or on the cage for them to hide. Remove cage skirts and seal off crevices, even tiny ones, such as where the wrought iron has been rolled to form a lip on the cage trays. Newspaper stacks should be secured in plastic tubs, rather than giving roaches a place to hide.

If you keep any seed on hand, remember to freeze it before you feed it to kill off those pesky moths.

Maintaining a clean birdcage is the best way to keep your home smelling fresh. However, there are creative ways to freshen the air in your home without endangering your parrot. Periodically, to add a little spice to everyone's life, I give my parrots cinnamon sticks as food toys. They shred them into tiny bits and throw them on the floor. Soon the house smells like cinnamon, especially when I vacuum up the bits. The cinnamon pieces in the vacuum bag leave the house smelling lovely every time I perform this chore. You can also add a nice aroma to your home by simmering a pan of water with ginger, cinnamon, and cloves. Don't forget fresh or dried nonpoisonous flowers as well, like lavender, an attractive, safe, and lovely-smelling flower.

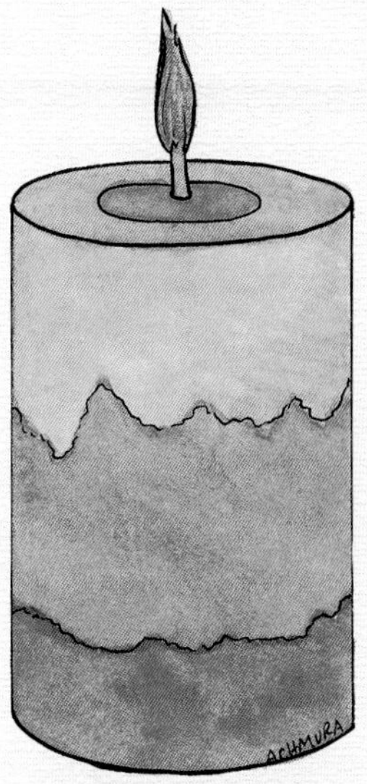

Scented candles, incense, and air fresheners can damage a parrot's delicate lungs.

Another way to keep your house smelling fresh is with an air purifier. If your parrot is a particularly dusty one, such as a cockatoo or an African grey, an air purifier can be helpful with the dusting as well. It will clean the dust out of the air, keeping it off your furniture and out of your lungs. If you or your visitors have allergies, this can be extremely helpful, although a good purifier can be expensive. An alternative way to deal with the dust and keep the air fresh is to replace your central air filter with a HEPA filter designed to catch small particles. Leave the fan on and the filter will catch most of the particulates in the air.

Chapter 3

Feed the Birds:
NUTRITION

Now that you have your new parrot's digs in place, do you know what to feed her? The science of avian nutrition has evolved a great deal in the last ten years, but controversy still exists. Most professionals agree that an all-seed diet for the majority of parrots is a recipe for malnutrition and obesity. (Some of the species that live primarily on seed in the wild, like budgies, cockatiels, and lovebirds, may be better off eating primarily seed.) However, even the experts aren't so sure about pelleted diets. Pelleted diets are the parrot equivalent of dog or cat kibble and are relatively new on the market.

The problem mainly derives from the fact that different species of parrots have different nutritional requirements. There is no perfect pellet diet for all parrots. Some parrots, such as the hyacinth macaw who feeds primarily on Brazil nuts, have a highly specialized diet. Some birds need more calcium; others need more or less protein, but they all could benefit from a balanced and varied diet.

Pellets can be a suitable diet if they are supplemented with fruits, vegetables, legumes, grains, nuts, and seeds. You can share small amounts of food from the table with your bird and find many great recipes for healthy parrot treats. Feeding your bird a healthy, balanced diet does not have to be time consuming or expensive, either. There are many great ways to keep your food budget reasonable.

Some parrots, such as hyacinth macaws, need a specialized diet.

Safety First

When figuring out your bird's diet, keep safety foremost in your mind. Store foods properly to avoid spoilage. Scrub vegetables and remove outer layers if they are not organically grown. Don't leave food that could spoil in your bird's cage for more than a couple hours. Lastly, but most importantly, don't ever feed your parrot anything new without first determining if it is poisonous.

If you're a healthy eater, some of the best and most fun inexpensive snacks for your parrot might come from your refrigerator. Remember, though, to never give your parrot avocado, chocolate, alcohol, or caffeinated drinks. If it isn't good for you, it most certainly isn't good for your parrot, so fried foods, salts, and so on are out. Don't be afraid to give your parrot a new treat, but educate yourself first!

Pellets on a Budget

If pellets are the main component in your bird's diet, then they compose the majority of your parrot food funds. Don't seek out the cheapest pellets, though. Instead, do your homework and choose the parrot pellets that seem to have the best nutrition for your bird. Buy the best for your bird and then look for other ways to save money.

Pellets come in two forms: compressed and extruded. Compressed pellets are created by heating the finely ground ingredients with steam. The mix is then compressed into a

Five Healthy Components of Your Parrot's Daily Diet

5

1. Fruits
2. Vegetables
3. Grains and some seed
4. Pellets
5. Fresh water

The special sixth component is variety. Feed your bird the widest variety of foods possible, and she'll most likely be healthy and happy.

pellet. Extruded pellets are cooked under pressure at a much higher heat. At these temperatures, any bacteria are destroyed—unlike at the lower temperatures at which compressed pellets are cooked—but some of the vitamins are also destroyed. Extruded pellets are also much denser than compressed pellets.

Choosing a pellet will have to be a personal decision. I suggest reading the ingredients and comparing the various pellets, as well as asking your vet what he or she suggests. Most of the parrot food companies will send you small sample bags of their products if you request them, which is another great way to compare. You may even want to taste them yourself. If you think one pellet tastes best, your parrot may agree.

Pellets are an important part of your parrot's diet, so buy the most nutritious brand you can find.

Buying pellets in bulk is a wonderful way to save money. You can often spend less by purchasing a 20-pound (9 kg) bag of food instead of buying multiple 2-pound (0.9 kg) bags. The large bag may seem unwieldy, but it's well worth the effort. Simply store the majority of the bag in a large airtight container in your refrigerator, and dip into this stash when the container you feed out of gets low. If you don't have much refrigerator room, break the bag up into storage bags that will feed your flock for a week, and store them in the freezer. The shelf life of pellets will be extended when kept refrigerated or frozen, but the length of time they will stay fresh will depend on whether or not they contain preservatives. Be sure to note the expiration date on the bag, and mark your stash of pellets with the date. Always smell or even taste pellets before feeding them to your parrot to ensure freshness.

Don't waste any of your pellets, either. When you get to the bottom of your bag, resist the temptation to throw the extras out with the dust. Get a colander and sift the remaining pellets out of the powder that remains. Every little bit counts, especially if your parrot's favorite form of fun is throwing her pellets on the floor. The leftover dust can be sprinkled on wet foods for extra flavor and nutrition.

Nuts

Parrot pellets are not the only item that can be bought in bulk. Whole nuts are an excellent addition to any parrot's diet as a treat and as a beak tamer. Nuts, such as almonds, can get expensive and aren't readily available all year. However, owners can purchase their parrot's

Join a Bird Club…or Start One!

If you only have one parrot and worry that buying in bulk might be a bit much, make some parront friends! Bird clubs can be a wonderful resource. A group of you might be able to buy in bulk, sharing the bounty and the cost. You can buy toy pieces in bulk and have a toy-making party. Perhaps you could even have a baking party for your gourmet parrots, sharing the expense, effort, and of course, the fun! Knowing other folks who care for a parrot of the same species can be extremely helpful in sharing information as well. For example, if you've noticed that lately your African grey has been flicking his toenails with his beak, you can ask another grey owner if his or her feathered friend has a similar behavior. You'll find that most greys flick their nails when they are anxious about something and then be better able to read your own bird. Of course, you'll also make new friends who share your passion for the feathered life. The new friendships will be rewarding for both you and your parrot.

favorite nuts in bulk from one of several online nut distributors and have them shipped straight to their home. Once the nuts arrive, they can be stored in the freezer until needed.

If you do buy nuts and other food items in bulk, purchase human-grade, high-quality food items. Purchasing nuts that are approved for animal consumption but not for humans can be dangerous, because they may be moldy and stale. In short, never feed your parrot foods that you wouldn't give your children or eat yourself.

Nuts are an important part of a balanced parrot diet.

Mold can be found on many nuts, especially peanuts. Dusty pellets, seeds, nuts, and spoiled fruits can harbor *Aspergillus*, a common mold that is found almost everywhere. Most birds and people can tolerate some mold in their environment, but a bird with a weakened immune system can easily succumb to aspergillosis, a dangerous infection of the respiratory system caused by this mold. Peanut shells are notorious for carrying *Aspergillus*, as well as toxins produced by the mold. Shelled, roasted, unsalted peanuts are best if you feel that you must include peanuts in your bird's diet. However, many avian vets feel that peanuts should be completely avoided.

Feeding Seeds

Seeds are a nice addition to a parrot's diet, but they should only make up 25 percent of her daily food. Most seeds are empty calories and not much more than junk food. As mentioned earlier, a few species of parrots, such as budgies and cockatiels, prefer seeds in their diet, but they should still eat extras like fruits and vegetables for better nutrition.

If you want to feed a mix with seeds as part of your bird's diet, look for one that contains minimal sunflower seeds or none at all. (Sunflower seeds have been linked to obesity and behavioral problems.) Also, choose a mix that is appropriate to your bird's size. Larger parrots are able to crack open larger seeds and nuts than smaller species can. In addition, always check your seed mix before feeding it. It should look clean, with no insects or rodent droppings, and it should smell fresh. Seeds can get rancid over time, so inspect the mix periodically. As with pellets, refrigerating seeds will extend their shelf life.

Sprouting Seeds

Sprouted seeds are a highly nutritious addition to any parrot's diet. Seeds for sprouting can be purchased from most bird supply stores. However, you can also purchase them from covered bulk bins at a health food store and create your own less expensive mix. Sunflower seeds, lentils, garbanzo beans, whole green peas, and even popcorn kernels can be sprouted, although popcorn will need to soak longer than other seeds. Avoid soybeans, lima beans, and kidney beans, which should be cooked instead of sprouted, and don't use seeds meant for planting.

To sprout seeds, rinse the mixture well, soak overnight, rinse again, and serve. A mason jar with cheese cloth secured with a rubber band on the top works well for this. The seeds don't need to have growth showing to be nutritious but can continue to be soaked and rinsed several times throughout the day for continued growth. Serve when short sprouts are showing. Be sure to sprout small batches to avoid spoilage. A tablespoon (15 ml) of sprouts is a generous serving.

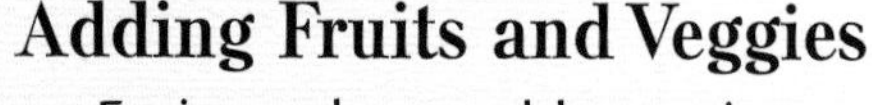

Adding Fruits and Veggies

Fruits and vegetables are important components of a varied parrot diet. In a pinch, defrosted frozen mixed vegetables work fine, but fresh produce has more nutrition and better texture. You should plan to get to know which grocery store in your area has the best produce available.

Just about all vegetables and fruits are good for your bird. The only produce you should avoid are avocado, rhubarb, and the pits and seeds of all fruit. Some people argue about the safety of all these items, but it is better to be safe than sorry. A few foods, such as celery and most lettuces, have little nutritional value, but even these are fine to feed once in a while. Still, keep up to date with any potentially toxic foods, and check sources you trust before feeding something new.

Feeding a wide variety of fruits and veggies will keep your parrot happy and healthy.

Today's produce does have one serious drawback—pesticides. Knowing that parrots are far more sensitive to poisons than humans, do the best you can to only feed organically grown produce. A few foods usually have low or no pesticide residue. These include corn, sweet potatoes, broccoli, and brussels sprouts. Even these should always be cleaned and the outer layers removed before you feed them to your parrot, though.

There are a few foods that you should never buy unless they are labeled "organically grown." These are plants that are highly susceptible to pests and therefore are almost always grown using lots of pesticides. They include strawberries, bell peppers, apples, spinach, green beans, and cucumbers. Unfortunately, this also means that they are difficult to grow organically, and the organic varieties can be much more expensive.

You can find organic produce at places other than the grocery store. If you have a local farmer's market, take a look. If some of the farmers are growing organic, not only will you be supporting local farming, but you will be getting fresher produce. Don't forget your neighbors' gardens, either. I was thrilled to see my new neighbors tending a backyard garden. My

Edible Flowers

In your quest to provide your parrot with a wide variety of foods, consider adding some edible flowers to her diet. Quite a few common flowers can be eaten, and some are highly nutritious. Their bright colors will draw your bird right to the food bowl. Left whole, the flowers double as toys that your parrot will toss around and shred as she eats. Here are a few types of flowers that are safe for your parrot:

- Carnations
- Clovers (high in several vitamins)
- Dandelions (high in vitamin A and calcium)
- Flowering herbs (such as basil, chives, cilantro, and sage)
- Hibiscus and Roses of Sharon (high in calcium)
- Marigolds
- Nasturtiums (high in calcium)
- Pansies
- Primroses
- Roses
- Sunflowers

If you are collecting these flowers from yards or parks, be absolutely sure that the areas aren't being sprayed with pesticides or other chemicals. Don't feed your bird flowers from a florist shop, either, because they are often treated to deter pests and extend freshness.

parrots dined on summer squash and jalapenos that my neighbors happily shared, along with pomegranates from a tree that we jointly tended at the fence line. Neighborhood gardens can be a boon, but just make sure no pesticides are used. Of course, if you want to be absolutely certain, you can always grow your own fruits and veggies.

A Parrot Garden

You can grow many healthy additions to your parrot's diet in your own garden. In fact, growing vegetables and greens for your bird is an excellent way to not only save a little money but also to ensure that your bird's food is free of pesticides. If you enjoy gardening, growing some tasty additions to everyone's meals can be a great use of a little spare time. Your wallet and your parrot will appreciate the effort.

Five Nutritious and Easy-to-Prepare Vegetables

5

1. Carrots: Cut into disks, spears, or chunks and leave the tops on.
2. Broccoli: Break apart or leave whole for large birds.
3. Cauliflower: Break apart or leave whole for large birds.
4. Chili Peppers: Just put in the bowl.
5. Peas: Put the whole pods in the bowl.

Many single-household folks have limited—if not nonexistent—gardening space. No problem! Container gardens are simple, easy to care for, and attractive. If you have a sunny porch, patio, or steps on which to set up pots, you can still grow a few goodies. Even a window container can work well. With so many people living in densely packed cities and apartments, seed companies are creating plants that are well suited to small spaces and container gardening. Look for plants that are described with words like "compact," "bush," and "space-saver."

Tomatoes are one of many vegetables you can grow in containers.

For the larger plants, such as tomatoes, use containers at least 12 inches (30 cm) deep. Make sure all your pots have holes for drainage, and drill your own if they do not. Choose soil that holds water well, with plenty of peat moss, perlite, or vermiculite, but you must still be prepared to water your containers more frequently than a regular garden. Plastic pots and wooden tubs will keep soil moist longer than hanging baskets or clay pots will, but they will still need to be watered every morning in the summer. The effort is well worth it, though, because a wide variety of vegetables can thrive in containers.

Peppers are a fabulous addition to a parrot's diet. They are high in vitamins A and C, as well as several minerals. They are also easy to grow in a pot placed in a sunny area. Bell peppers grow better in the ground, but the hot pepper varieties all thrive in pots. They can be planted in early spring and harvested in the summer. Grow as much as you have space for, because the thinner skinned hot peppers can be dried and stored in airtight containers. Don't worry if the peppers are too hot for you—your parrot won't mind the heat at all.

Many varieties of patio tomatoes are available as well, and these vegetables are a good source of vitamin A. They need to be planted in a sunny spot and can be mixed with pepper plants to save space or just to create an attractive pot. Be sure to stake your tomato plants to support the heavy fruit you're sure to harvest.

Broccoli is a great vegetable to grow for your bird because it provides vitamin A, vitamin C, and riboflavin. You can grow the plants in a rectangular container, and in hotter climates, they can be grown in the winter as well as the summer. Broccoli can tolerate some shade in hot weather, but in cooler temperatures, it should be grown in a sunny area.

Many parrots enjoy hot peppers.

Lettuce and cabbage can also do well in containers, but choose the darker green varieties because they contain the most nutrients. Iceberg lettuce has nearly no nutritional value. You can even try growing cabbage in hanging baskets. Just be sure to select the appropriate variety for your climate and the time of year.

You can also grow root vegetables like sweet potatoes, beets, and carrots, which are all highly nutritious and can be stored in a cool place for months. Choose the "nugget" type of carrots that aren't as long rooted. These vegetables can be grown in 9-inch-deep (23- cm) containers.

These are only a few of the possibilities for growing container vegetable gardens. If you have an area that receives about six hours of sun a day, you can grow just about any of the smaller varieties of vegetables. You can create a very striking space, especially if you throw in a few flowering plants. This will add a splash of color and also attract pollinating insects. Of

Bobbi's Birdie Bread

Cooking for the birds is fun and appreciated, so try this great recipe. It comes courtesy of Bobbi Brinker, longtime parrot breeder and author of *For the Love of Greys.*

- 2 boxes of corn muffin mix, such as Jiffy
- 3 tablespoons (15 ml)of baking powder
- 1 teaspoon (5 ml) spirulina powder (optional)
- 2 eggs with shells (pureed in blender)
- 4 4-ounce (118 ml) jars of fruit baby food, any flavor
- 3/4 cup (175 ml) of peanut butter
- 2 cups (500 ml) dry baby cereal
- 1 1/2 cups (355 ml) of shredded/chopped broccoli and carrots

Mix wet and dry ingredients separately. Combine all ingredients. Spray a 9 x 13-inch (23 x 33-cm) pan with cooking spray. Bake for 30 minutes at 400°F (204°C). Check to see if firm in the middle. Cool, cut into squares, and freeze in freezer bags for future use. Defrost as needed.

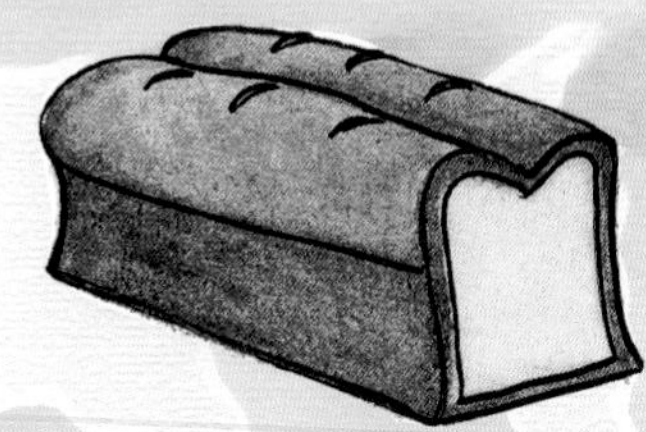

course, if you have a plot of land—even a small one—your possibilities are virtually limitless. You can even try growing beans and corn, which are both easy to store and excellent for cooked diets.

Don't give your parrot chocolate, avocados, salty snacks, or fatty foods.

Cooking for the Birds

Bean mixes provide an excellent way to add a little more nutrition and variety into your bird's diet. If time is of the essence, you can purchase pre-mixed parrot diets, such as Crazy Corn and Dr. Harvey's Veg-to-Bowl. However, it's simple and inexpensive to create your own bean mix. Purchase a bag of 15 bean soup mix, soak overnight, and add a few extras when you boil. You can throw in whole-grain pasta, some dried peppers, or whatever variety of treats works best for your bird. Once you've cooked the mixture, store it in a small container that equals no more than four days of servings. Just thaw and serve. Store the thawed mix in the refrigerator, but be sure to check it, because it can spoil rapidly.

If you do a little research, you will find that recipes for your bird are limitless. Aim for variety in nutrition, texture, and taste, and get in the habit of giving your bird an assortment of foods from the start. A young bird who has been given many different edible treasures will be more likely to try new treats as an older bird. You just may find your own diet becoming healthier as you shop for and cook meals that work for both of you.

Eating From the Table

Sharing "people food" can be fine if there are healthy foods on your plate. When I was doing bird shows with an enigmatic little African grey named Quazar, I frequently had people come up and tell me stories about their greys. Whenever I heard about a particularly long-lived grey, I would ask what she had been fed. Avian nutrition was a particularly hot topic at this time because seed diets were considered "out," and the new pellet diets were being recommended. As a result, I was very interested in what these people had to say. I wasn't surprised to hear that these antiquarian greys were fed a steady diet from the table—generally rice, beans, pasta, and produce. Table food can certainly be nutritious, and feeding your bird from the table can become a fun social event. In my house, if I'm eating, everybody's eating, and this is our quality time. You should enjoy your mealtime as flock time.

Cooking meals for your bird is rewarding for both of you.

How Much To Feed?

Trying to decide exactly what and how much to feed your parrot requires that you do your homework. Thoughts on diet are constantly changing. Talk to avian vets and breeders who specialize in your parrot's species to get the best dietary information for her specific species. If you have an eclectus, for example, a breeder who specializes in eclectus parrots will have very clear ideas about nutrition, having raised babies successfully and perhaps learned from mistakes. He or she will know what diets kept babies from being stunted or having other growth problems and will be happy to pass on this information to you.

Fight the bird bulge: Don't overfeed your parrot.

Generally speaking, you should provide a parrot with pellets and fresh water all day. You can serve fresh vegetables and fruits, grains, legumes, whole-grain pasta, and nuts twice a day at breakfast and dinner. Provide these items in a large quantity, but only just large enough that your parrot will finish most of them in one sitting. Finally, be mindful of fatty foods, and know that bored parrots will overeat.

Obesity

Obesity has become a problem with many pet parrots, especially Amazon parrots. Overweight birds will stand with a wider stance, have bald patches where feather tracts have separated due to excess layers of fat below the skin, and perhaps feature a roll of fat under the chin. Parrot owners should be mindful of obesity as a serious health problem in parrots. Some veterinarians note that most parrots are overfed or fed diets that are too high in fat or processed fatty table scraps.

To avoid obesity in your parrot, make sure that she receives plenty of exercise. Your bird should have climbing time and get plenty of exercise on her play gym. Even moving the water bowl to the other side of the cage, away from the food bowl, can be helpful. You should also consider getting a scale with a perch so that you can teach your parrot to sit calmly while you weigh her. You'll be able to note weight gain or any weight loss that may signify illness. Of course, annual checkups at the vet can help avoid dietary problems as well.

Chapter 4

Bringing Home Baby: ADJUSTING TO YOUR NEW PARROT AND VICE VERSA

Now that your parrot paradise is set up and you have an avian feast prepared, it's time to bring home your new friend. This is a fun and important time, whether your parrot is a youngster or a rescue about to find her final home. If you are observant, thoughtful, and patient with your parrot, you will cement the foundation of a wonderful lifelong relationship.

Your first few weeks may be a little stressful, but try to have fun. This is when you and your parrot figure out what your life together is going to be like. Your parrot will watch you closely to discover what to expect, when you might be on your way to offer a treat, when playtime happens, and what you consider appropriate interaction. You should learn from your bird as well. Realize when your parrot is telling you she wants to be left alone; for example, does she put her head down, move to the back of the cage, or maybe turn her back to you? Also, discover what foods and toys she likes best. Does she destroy anything made of pine, or does she become really animated at the possibility of an almond in her bowl? Most importantly, keep your interactions positive, and let your parrot make choices. Don't ever "make" your parrot do anything or take her trust in you for granted.

If your parrot turns her back to you, she probably wants to be left alone.

When determining your parrot's preferences, first figure out what she considers her favorite treat. If you know what your parrot likes to nibble on best—maybe something like almonds or pine nuts—you can leave that one treat out of the daily meals and use it as a reward or just as a way to build your friendship. Some parrots respond to toys and affection, but using a treat as a reward is more straightforward. Don't use food as starvation or trickery. Parrots share food in the wild—they eat together in flocks and regurgitate for their mates. Giving your parrot a treat for going back in her cage or stepping up onto your hand makes communication easier and helps to strengthen your bond.

Acclimating Your New Bird

Take care when acclimating your parrot to her new environment. The first few days should be quiet. This week might not be the best time to have your young nieces and nephews over for a visit or to have a big party. Your parrot needs time to take in her new surroundings and become comfortable with them.

Be prepared for some things to make your parrot nervous in her new home. Hopefully, you've chosen a place for your parrot's cage that allows for easy interaction but isn't directly in the path of many new scary things. For example, if you're

Five Things to Introduce to a New Parrot

Always take care that new things don't frighten your parrot and take your time introducing them to your bird. Here are five things you should acclimate your parrot to:

1. A variety of treats
2. Daily routines
3. Different toys
4. Members of the household
5. Visiting friends

having furniture delivered, you probably don't want the delivery folks walking a big couch right by the cage. You might find that your bird is afraid of brooms, funny hats, or even a brightly colored blanket.

Watch your new friend closely as you introduce new household objects. Some parrots are completely fearless, and others need a chance to see things from a distance and convince themselves that there's nothing to fear. A nervous parrot will slick down her feathers, lean away, and move her body like she would take flight if she could. A flighted bird might simply fly away, or a caged parrot might flee to the back of the cage. Learn this body language so that you are sensitive to things that make your parrot react negatively.

Consistency and change, although seemingly contradictory, are two very important aspects to introduce to a new parrot. Parrot owners who are extremely consistent in their communication and behavior around their bird will be successful in building a strong relationship. As a result, make an effort to be consistent in all your interactions. Say the same thing when you remove the dishes from your bird's cage or any other daily interaction, and use the exact same cue for everything you ask. If you say "up" when asking your parrot to step up, then always use this same cue. Make sure that you hold your hand in the same position as well. Be consistent at saying "good" at the exact moment your parrot does what you are asking, and always offer a treat or other positive reinforcement afterward. When you are consistent like this, you become less of an untrustworthy mystery to your parrot. They are not little people, and parrot owners don't look or act like parrots (even though we try very hard), so consistency is the best bridge between our species.

Another important aspect to molding a well-adjusted parrot is a changing environment. This may sound like the opposite of consistency, but an environment that changes can help your parrot learn how to react to new things. Parrots who live in the same corner of the room with the same toys, interacting with the same people in a never-changing world, will display nervous behavior when things suddenly look different. At some point, things are going to change, so parrot owners should make sure that their feathered friends are up to dealing with adjustment. If it's possible, move your parrot's cage to other places in the room from time to time. Constantly and carefully introduce new toys, new foods, new people, and new sounds. Again, be very careful to ensure that the situation always remains positive, but get your

Some trainers advocate leaving parrots flighted, while other advocate clipping.

parrot used to change from the beginning. Some of the most well-adjusted parrots I've met belonged to young people who acquired their pets before they were settled. Those parrots have been moved time and time again and aren't bothered in the least when their environment changes. A fun and adventurous parrot is certainly a treat to have as a friend.

Winging It: To Clip or Not To Clip

When parrot owners talk about adventurous parrots, discussion of free-flight and wing clipping often comes up. Several schools of thought exist on whether or not to clip. Again, do your homework. There are pros and cons to each argument, and parrot owners should make a careful and well-informed decision.

Some avian behavior consultants and veterinarians believe that parrots should be allowed to fly for their physiological and mental well-being. They feel that flighted parrots are better adjusted and that flying assists in keeping them internally healthy. Some parrot owners insist that birds were meant to fly and refuse to clip their parrot's wings.

The arguments for allowing parrots to fly are valid, but the thoughts on clipping are valid as well. Flighted parrots are more likely to get themselves into trouble by flying into ceiling fans, fireplaces, or pots boiling on top of the stove. It also only takes one instance of leaving a door open to the

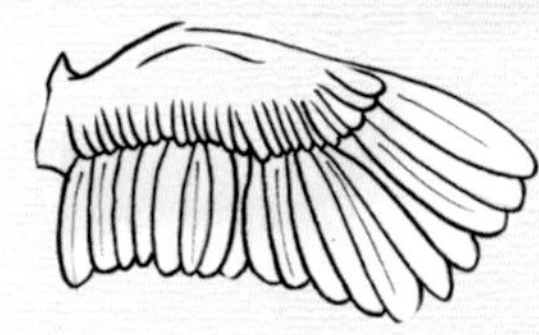

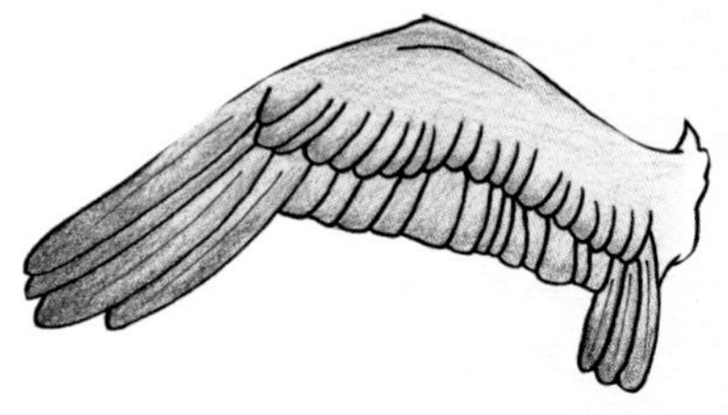

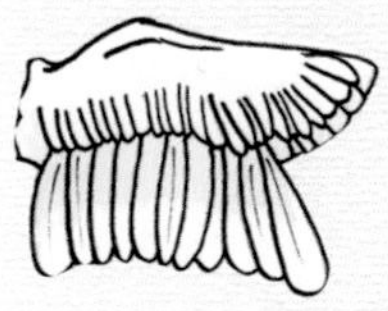

Wing clipping consists of removing just enough feathers to inhibit flight.

outside for a bird to fly away, and parrots often don't survive if they manage to get outside. Smaller parrots encounter myriad predators, and most don't have the flight skills or training to make their way back to their owner.

Many breeders now encourage parrot owners to at least allow their birds to learn to fly (fledging) as youngsters before they clip their wings. Birds who have learned to fly seem to be more poised and confident, moving about less awkwardly than birds who never learned to fly. This seems to be especially important with the more heavy-bodied parrots, like African greys. Before clipping, your bird should be able to fly proficiently, both up and down, as well as land. Experts who believe in fledging parrots feel that it should be a time

Dangerous Toy Pieces

Here's a list of toys and toy parts that are dangerous for your bird and should never be used as playthings:

- Any metal that contains zinc (stainless steel and powder-coated metal are safest)
- Bells with clappers
- Brittle plastic that can be broken into small pieces and swallowed
- Chemically treated wood or leather
- Frayed and stringy rope
- Jingle bells
- Key rings
- Pieces colored with anything other than vegetable dye
- Toys that are too small for your bird

of extreme caution, however. Birds who are just learning how to fly are awkward and easily get into dangerous situations. A baby bird should be kept out of trouble as she learns to fly, and then she should be clipped.

I've free-flown birds for more than a decade in shows and as a falconer. I've had many birds fly off and almost always gotten them back, but my parrots at home are clipped. I see value in both sides of this argument but don't feel confident that I can keep my parrots safe if they are flighted. This is a personal decision, so be sure to make it carefully.

Home Alone: Latchkey Parrots

In a single-person household, chances are good that the parrot is going to spend a portion of her time alone. If you work at home, like I'm fortunate enough to do now, you're in great shape, although I have to admit, I sometimes think my parrots wish I would go away for a while, especially when my African grey launches into a half hour of "goodbyes" when I'm not planning to go anywhere. In the past, my parrots managed through my 40- to 50-hour-a-week absences, but they got every moment I could give them when I wasn't working. Many of my friends were professional bird trainers who owned parrots, and at social events, most of us cut out early to get home to our "kids." You should plan to do the same—this is a lifestyle commitment.

If you work full-time outside of the house, you should spend as much of your free time as possible at home. Consider becoming the primary host or hostess in your social group. By moving parties, movie nights, and other gatherings to your home, your parrot can be a part of the "flock" as much as possible. Give your bird as much attention as you can routinely provide. Set the bar for the most hours you think you can give your bird on a daily basis, and stick to it. She will come to expect her allotted playtime, and hopefully, it will become the best part of your day.

If you forget to lock your parrot's cage, you could come home to a scene like this!

Parrot Entertainment

If you work all day, you will need ways to keep your feathered friend happy and content until you can come home and give her some attention. Here are a few ideas for entertaining your parrot while you're not home.

- Call home and leave a message on your answering machine for your bird
- Have plenty of toys inside the cage and exchange new toys for old ones frequently
- Have the radio playing on a soft jazz, classical, or talk station
- Provide foraging opportunities for your bird (see the sidebar in this chapter)

Home-Alone Safety

If your parrot is going to have to spend some time at home alone, make sure that she's going to stay safe and sound. This means that a parrot should not be allowed to roam free when you're away unless she's in a room that has been prepared with her safety in mind. Your parrot may never seem to get into trouble in the living room, but you would be amazed by what fun a restless beak finds when no one is supervising (not to mention the destruction that beak can wreak). The safest place for a home-alone parrot is usually in her cage or in a specially prepared bird room.

Keep a close watch for dangers in the cage as well. Pay attention to fraying toys that can entangle your bird. Don't leave food that easily spoils in the cage all day. If your parrot proves to be an escape artist, make sure that doors are secured by small padlocks or other means. Many a cockatoo has let herself out of the cage and into an amazing amount of trouble. Don't forget the danger of rushing off to work and forgetting to shut a cage door, either. I once forgot to shut my Senegal in the cage before I left for work and returned to such mass destruction that I was more awed than angry. Remember to make sure that your bird's cage is secured every day before you leave for work!

If your parrot shares her home with other animals, they should be separated while you're gone. Too many parrots have been pulled through cage bars, bitten, or clawed. It only takes one scratch or nip from a cat to kill your bird, because the bacteria in a cat's claws and mouth will quickly make the wound septic. By the time your parrot looks sick, it will be too late. If you don't know your parrot has been injured and fail to quickly get her on antibiotics, she will die. It is much better to play it safe.

Toys

If you're going to have to leave your parrot for more than a few hours, make certain that your feathered busybody has plenty to do. Toys are a critical part of a well-adjusted parrot's life, and they should be abundant and imaginative. In fact, even if you're home all day every day, your parrot should have active feet and a busy beak.

Toys are generally designed for three types of birds: noisemakers, thinkers, and chewers.

Safety comes first when you are looking at toys, so before you put a new toy in your bird's cage, make certain that it is harmless. If it's edible, scrutinize the ingredients and make sure that you don't accidentally poison your bird. Check for small pieces that can be pulled off and choke your bird or become stuck on her beak. Avoid jingle bells, zinc, metal pieces with unwelded openings, and key rings.

Periodically inspect old toys for damage. If you use cloth or rope, make sure that there are no threads that can get wrapped around a bird's toe. We've all heard many sad stories about birds who have injured or killed themselves while their owners were away. Remember, parrots are easily stressed, and a parrot in distress for a long period of time could suffer long-term damage (mental and physical) or die. However, a little bit of common sense is a lifesaver. Don't be obsessive, but be sure to give your toys a little thought.

Today, parrot toys are easy to find. A tremendous number of resources exist on the Internet for mail-order playthings. Toys can also be found at your local independent or

Five Quick Parrot Toys

Here are five easy, inexpensive toys to give your parrot:

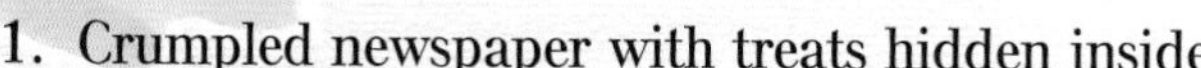

1. Crumpled newspaper with treats hidden inside
2. Empty cereal boxes with treats or toys hidden inside
2. Empty paper towel rolls stuffed with shredded newspaper
4. Shredded newspaper woven through cage bars
5. Tongue depressors for chewing and waving around

franchise pet store. They come in an enormous variety and are made for various sizes of birds. All you need to do is choose the best fit for your bird.

Parrot toys often include ladders, bells, ropes, and chewable wooden parts.

Generally, toys are designed for three types of players: chewers, noisemakers, and thinkers. Chewers like toys that can be shredded, stripped, and broken down into tiny remains. Noisemakers like toys that ring, sing, clang, and bang. Thinkers like puzzle toys that require time and effort to remove a treat or other interesting bit. However, all birds can and should be taught to interact with all three kinds of toys—so don't forget to give a thinker something to chew on, for example. We all like to do something a little different and crazy now and then. Tastes change, too, so keep in mind that your parrot might just switch her favorites.

Inexpensive Toys

Buying a lot of parrot toys can get expensive, but don't despair. Many good resources are available for inexpensive toys. A great place to find cheap toys is at craft stores. Tongue depressors and wood pieces from the craft store are inexpensive items that provide wonderful fun for a small chewer. Household items can be inventive toys as well. For example, used paperback romances and

Tools of the Toy-Making Trade

It doesn't take much time and effort to make parrot toys similar to those you can buy in the store. I highly recommend purchasing a high-quality power drill as a part of your tool kit. You will use it for myriad parrot-entertaining endeavors. A block of untreated pine and a drill can be many a wondrous thing for a parrot. Drill some holes in the wood and hide pine nuts, almonds, tongue depressors, and many other fun finds. Drill a hole in the corner and you can attach it to the cage with a quick link. You can purchase plenty of toy-making pieces and make them into a multitude of delights with a little imagination. Try a combination of any of these items:

- Clothespins
- Cowbells
- Dried fruit (sulfur free)
- Naturally tanned leather strips
- Penne pasta (or other shapes)
- Pony beads
- Sisal rope
- Stainless steel quick links
- Straws
- Whiffle balls
- Wooden spools

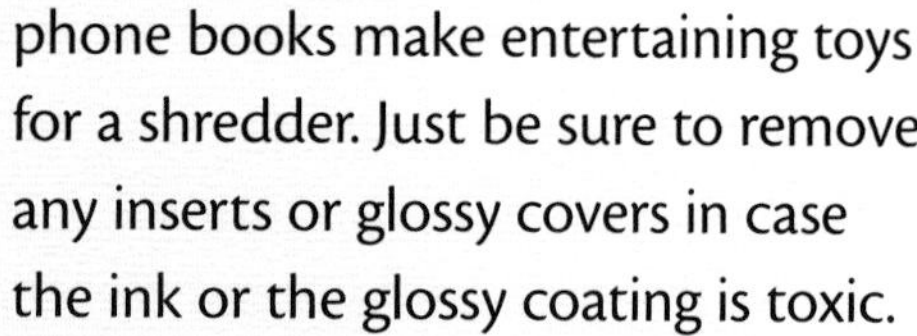

phone books make entertaining toys for a shredder. Just be sure to remove any inserts or glossy covers in case the ink or the glossy coating is toxic.

Pinecones make great toys. Collect, disinfect, and bake them at 250°F (121°C) for 30 minutes. I like to gather cholla skeletons in the desert near my house. I disinfect and cook them, just like the pinecones, and stuff the cholla with pine nuts and other interesting bits. Just keep using your imagination! Pet stores often sell cholla skeletons, usually in the reptile supply section. They should still be disinfected, just as if you found them outdoors.

Check your favorite stores and websites for sales as well. You can often find discontinued parrot toys discounted at major pet stores. The toy might not have been a best seller, but it may just make the perfect toy for your parrot. Just be sure that the toy is well made and won't turn into a hazard. You can also watch your favorite toy suppliers for discounts on larger quantities of toys. If a particular type of toy is a hit with your parrot, you can purchase several at a discounted price.

Making toys not only saves you money but can be fun for you as well as your bird. You don't have to get complicated. Toys can be as simple as one designed from a leftover cereal or cookie box. Just tear off a few flaps and voila—you have a Senegal parrot fun fest! Getting creative with a hanging metal kebab is easy, too. Just add a few dried peppers or fruit and some pasta shapes with holes in them, and you have an instant toy. Try stuffing an empty paper towel roll with some newspaper shreddings and shoving it between the cage bars. This is a hit with many mess-making parrots.

If you have the knack for toy making, you can get super creative and have even more fun. It's not hard to recycle old bits of toys into new ones. An industrious parrot owner can even make complicated toys by buying drilled wood, leather, and plastic pieces. Many places exist where toy parts can be purchased and assembled into the perfect toy at home.

Large parrots, such as green-winged macaws, need larger and sturdier toys than smaller species.

The best way to retain an inexpensive stock of toys is to keep a storage container full of them. Once you have a chest of toys, you won't have to constantly buy new ones. Just rotate toys through your bird's cage from your stockpile, and replace or rejuvenate them as they get worn out. This way, you always have toys on hand and can be sure that your parrot is not getting bored with the playthings in her cage. This is part of a process called enrichment and can make a huge difference in your parrot's life.

Without enough enrichment, your parrot could become depressed.

Enrich Me!

Do you feel like you live in a zoo? Maybe you should run your house like you own a zoo! All accredited zoos in North America are required to have ongoing enrichment programs for their animals, including their birds. This is because all wild animals need to be stimulated mentally in ways that simulate wild behavior. Without enrichment, cats pace, birds overpreen, and many intelligent animals become depressed. The American Zoo and Aquarium Association (AZA) defines enrichment as "a process for improving or enhancing animal environments and care within the context of their inhabitants' behavioral biology and natural history." Basically, it is giving an animal the opportunity to engage in activities it might normally do in the wild.

Enrichment programs are simple, and anyone can implement them in his or her own home. These programs only have three rules: ensure safety, use your imagination, and make it fun for everyone.

Enrichment only works if it is constantly changing, so now that you have safety in mind, it's time to come up with a plan. At zoos, enrichment items are moved out of animal enclosures every couple of days. You may want to notice how your parrot interacts with new toys and decide how often to change up playthings based on your own bird. Parrots sometimes need to have a new toy in their cage several days before they will even explore it. On the other hand, chewable toys may be annihilated by a boisterous cockatoo in one day. Decide what works best for your bird, and mark a calendar or pick a set day every week and change a toy in your bird's cage. Make sure to change up the types of toys, too. The more change, the better!

However, if you have a parrot who is new to enrichment or who is always nervous with new things, take it slow. If your bird throws herself around the cage, cowers in the corner, or even just freezes, unable to take her eyes off the new "intruder" in her cage, then take care

Foraging for Fun

In the wild, food doesn't arrive in a bowl, and there's no reason that your parrot's entire meal should, either. In fact, studies have shown that animals will ignore a bowl of free food for the same food placed in such a way that the animal is able to engage in a learned behavior to get it.

There are hundreds of ways to set up your parrot's cage so that finding food is fun and exciting. You can buy tiny boxes at craft stores to hide nuts and fruits. Other ideas include rolling up treats in newspaper, tying up treats in packages, putting treats inside deli containers, and placing a few tidbits under newspaper on the cage floor. You can purchase acrylic toys, such as round cages and pyramids, that hide treats and are designed to encourage foraging. In addition, you can place greens and vegetables throughout the cage with clips and kebobs. The more time your parrot spends thinking, searching, and playing while she eats, the happier she'll be.

introducing toys. Don't give up, though; just give her a chance to get over her fears. Put the new toy out where your bird can see it for a couple of days, and every day, move it closer to the cage. Try hanging it outside of the cage for a while, and when your bird is comfortable with it, hang the toy inside. Watch for clutter, too, because a maze of toys in the cage may not be fun for your parrot. Try putting in just a few, leaving plenty of wing room.

It's Their Job

Now that you have a plan, it's time to decide what sort of toys you should use. Here's where your imagination comes in. What does your parrot like to do most? What is she doing when she gets into trouble (obviously something she enjoys)? What might your parrot be doing in the wild, and what can you do to simulate this activity? If your parrot doesn't play, then what can you teach her to play with?

Some things that serve as enrichment might surprise you. My parrots throw paper and wood chips from annihilated toys on the floor every day. When visitors comment on my mess-making birds, I often retort, "Well, it's their job!" And it is their job. Dropping bits of plants that include seeds on the forest floor is a parrot's job as nature's gardener, so let your bird make a mess. In fact, help her make a mess! Does your parrot like to rip up the newspaper at the bottom of her cage? Buy toys that are designed to be shredded, or weave bits of newspaper through the cage bars one day and let your bird shred away. Is your parrot looking for something in which to chew a nesting hollow? If so, give her a nice chunk of untreated pine or a soft pine toy.

Setting up an environment that encourages foraging is one way to help a parrot keep occupied during the day. Parrots in the wild thrive on very diverse diets, and they spend a decent part of their day foraging and taking advantage of whatever is available or in season. Foraging behavior also acts as a social stimulus, allowing parrots to interact as well as explore and otherwise occupy their minds. Providing a similar edible environment for your parrot can assist in keeping her happy and well behaved.

If your bird likes water, spend some quality time in the shower with her.

When you are home, make sure that you use your time wisely with your parrot. Find ways to be involved with her while you do your chores and prepare for the next day. Bring your bird to sit on the shower door or curtain rod while you shower. Sing her a song while you do the dishes. And be sure to set aside some chunks of time every day to get in some training, because training your parrot is a wonderful way to build and maintain a positive relationship. If you spend a little time training every day, you'll be more prepared to think through and manage problem behaviors when they arise.

Chapter 5

Oh, Behave!: THE WELL-ADJUSTED PARROT

Training isn't making animals do "things." Training is forging a bond and learning to communicate clearly in an interspecies relationship. If you want the most fulfilling relationship possible with your parrot, learn to be a bird trainer.

Training Talk: Positive Reinforcement

Positive reinforcement is the presentation of a stimulus following a behavior that serves to maintain or increase the frequency of that behavior. Basically, it is training through rewards. Giving the reward increases the likelihood that the subject will perform the desired behavior. Positive reinforcers are usually things that the learner finds enjoyable and pleasant; with parrots, a small piece of food is the usual reinforcer. When using this training technique, the learner tends to exceed the effort necessary to obtain the award. Positive reinforcement is the best way to train a parrot.

Parrot owners who can teach their bird to speak, raise her wings, or turn around on cue can teach their bird to do just about anything. A trained parrot has been taught to try to understand her human companion's requests, and—even more importantly—the human in the equation has learned to think a little like a parrot. Training birds isn't easy, but that's not because it's complicated. Training isn't easy because it takes a concerted effort and a lot of commitment. But it's also a tremendous amount of fun!

Positive Interactions and Reinforcement

The most important part of training a parrot is to keep every interaction with your bird positive. Again, parrots are not domestic animals, so your bird's bond with you isn't unconditional. A parrot who has a bad experience in the wild will only continue to survive if she avoids the experience in the future. Our gorgeously wild parrots bring this mentality to our

Try to make all interactions with your parrot positive.

homes. Keep in mind that your marriage to your parrot is delicate, and sometimes even one bad experience can make her distrust you.

Try to make sure that every time your parrot sees you, there is a positive interaction. If your parrot is unsure of you, carefully offer a treat when you walk by the cage. This will lead her to look forward to your appearance and the possibility of something tasty. Just make sure that your parrot is not doing something you don't want to reward when you walk by, like screaming. Every interaction should be positive, but you must always be mindful of ignoring bad behavior.

It's also important to ensure that you are not the center of uncomfortable experiences. My parrots are terrified of the seemingly innocuous and quiet faux-feather duster that I use. I suggest handling a problem similar to mine in the following way. (Simply replace the word "duster" with whatever object frightens your bird.) When you bring out the duster, if bird looks anxious or thrashes around in her cage, stop! Leave the duster out, but keep it far enough away not to be scary. Let your parrot adjust. Shake the duster once in a while, and move it around. Gradually dust closer to the cage until your parrot just doesn't care anymore. Take hours, days, or weeks to accomplish this—just don't make yourself into the evil person with that incredibly scary object. Then, use this technique of gradual introduction with anything else that frightens your bird.

Training with your parrot should, of course, be positive as well. Positive reinforcement should be the center of your training technique. This means that when your bird does something you desire, she gets a reward: a treat, a cuddle, or something else that she wants. Animals—including people—that are rewarded for desired behaviors will repeat them. In fact, they will work even harder to please. For example, if your boyfriend brings you a rose and you gush over the gift, telling him he's the best boyfriend ever, he may very well bring you a dozen next time. It's the same with a parrot. If your parrot learns that she gets rewarded for certain behaviors, she'll offer different and bigger behaviors, trying to figure out how to get your attention and the treat in your hand.

Positive reinforcement works so well that aversive punishment and negative reinforcement should not be used with a parrot. These techniques can work on the surface, but they have drawbacks. Negative reinforcement is something that the animal will work to avoid—for example, rubbing a stick on the back of a parrot's legs to get her to step up. The parrot will step up but only to make the stick stop rubbing her legs. An example of aversive punishment would be to squirt a bird with a spray bottle when she screams. I can guarantee the bird will only stop screaming when she sees the bottle. She isn't learning to stop screaming, though; she's learning to avoid spray bottles. These techniques also ruin relationships. Your parrot is going to become anxious whenever she sees a stick or a bottle, and you will end up with an unpredictable parrot who displays bad behaviors based on aggression and fear. There is no reason for this when these behaviors can be trained with positive reinforcement.

On the flip side of the coin, if you use positive reinforcement, your bird will be excited to work with you. If you train her to know that stepping up on a stick gets her a reward, she will be excited when she sees the stick. If you teach her to make another noise other than screaming, like a soft whistle, for a reward, she will offer

Training Talk: Event Markers

An event marker is a sound used to inform an animal that it just did what you wanted, and a treat is forthcoming. An event marker is a critical tool for anyone who wants to better communicate with an animal. It allows you to reward behavior the moment it occurs. For example, if you hear your bird wolf whistle from the other room and want to reward this, you can call out "good" as an event marker. If your bird always hears "good" before she is given a treat, she will understand that this whistle gets her a reward. If you don't use an event marker, by the time you get in the room with a treat, your parrot will have moved on to another behavior and you may end up rewarding an undesirable behavior.

Training Talk: Negative Reinforcement

Negative reinforcement is the removal of a stimulus following a behavior that serves to maintain or increase its frequency. It is often called avoidance training. The learner will only work as hard as is necessary to avoid the stimulus, which is generally unpleasant. An example would be holding up a towel or some other frightening object to herd a parrot into her crate. She will go in to avoid the stimulus of the frightening towel, but you've probably eroded your relationship. If you train with positive reinforcement, your bird will go in the crate just because she has a history of being rewarded for doing so.

the new sound over and over, hoping for a treat. Your bird will see you as a bringer of good things and fun times. Why would you want to train any differently?

Giving Parrots Choices

Humans have a tendency to assert dominance in relationships. Why not? It works well with other humans. Parrots are different, though. There's no dominance in a flock. Parrots with a disagreement don't battle it out for a place in the hierarchy—they simply fly away. With this in mind, don't try to make your parrot do anything, because you'll only cause her to distrust you.

The problem that many parrot owners have, however, is that they don't realize that they're forcing their parrots to do things. These incidences can be so tiny, like leaving your hand in front of your parrot and then nudging a little when she doesn't want to step up. If you learn to read your bird's body language and look for it, you'll see that she isn't interested in stepping up. Maybe she has moved to the back corner of the cage, or her feathers are slicked down and her head is bowed. If day after day you ignore your parrot's wishes and make her step up anyway, she's going to bite you at some point, and your relationship will only deteriorate from there.

If you train your bird with positive reinforcement, she will be eager to do what you are asking.

If you empower your parrot, you are certain to have a fantastic relationship. I know, it sounds a little crazy, but it really is what works best. Let your parrot have a choice. You want her to step on your hand, so offer her a treat. If she does it, she gets a reward. If she doesn't step up, you walk away, but forfeiting the treat was her choice. Parrots who are allowed to make their own decisions when there's a reward involved will quickly stop refusing. Don't worry; you won't create birdie bedlam. Give your parrot the power and she'll act like she's a part of the flock and work with you, not plot against you.

Parrots are so small that we forget that they want some control in their lives sometimes—we scoop them up, tote them around, and spray them down when they don't want a bath. Wild animals have more control over their environment, so empowering the wild parrots in our homes will stimulate them mentally and keep them well adjusted. Keep this in mind as you start to teach each other new tricks.

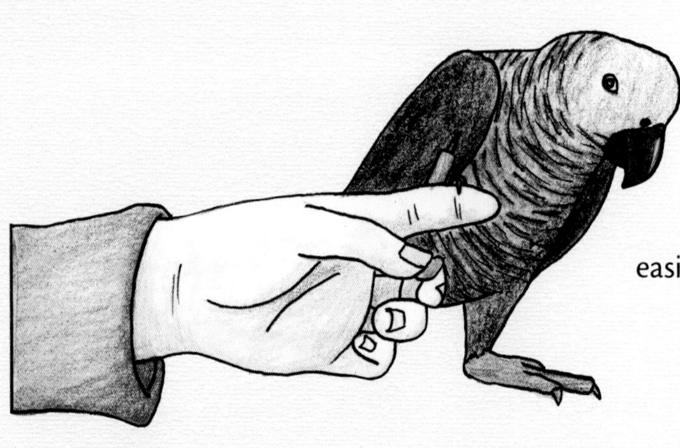

Training a parrot to step up requires patience.

Stepping Up

Stepping up is one of the most important behaviors that your parrot can learn and one of the easiest to teach. A parrot who steps up when asked to is more likely to have a healthy, interactive relationship with her owner. She can also be quickly removed from a dangerous situation. Plenty of good reasons exist to make sure your parrot is comfortable stepping up onto your hand.

Unfortunately, the way to train a bird to step up is often misunderstood. Knowing how important this behavior is, many owners force their birds to step up onto their hands. They feel this is the one thing their bird must do when asked. Owners with this attitude often suffer many bites, and some people even endure the pain, allowing their birds to bite and refusing to acknowledge this undesirable behavior. A parrot who knows that she will be bullied until she steps up will definitely perform the behavior, but there are some serious consequences to training in this manner.

Again, parrots who are forced to do things often have rocky relationships with their owners, and birds who have been pressured to step up in a new relationship may quickly develop fear aggression. If a parrot is even a little fearful of her owner, she may cower, bite, or scream. Other parrots may just slick down their feathers and try to ignore you when you approach them, knowing that you are going to make them do something they don't wish to do. A much better solution for both the owner and the parrot is to teach the bird that stepping up is rewarding.

Training a parrot to step up is very simple and only requires patience. Once you know what you are going to use as a treat, offer your open hand to the bird to step up on, and hand her the treat. Gradually get your bird to reach over your hand in order to get her treat. It is important to make sure that your bird is feeling comfortable and not nervous or anxious, because you want stepping up to be a pleasant experience. If this is a new parrot who doesn't know you yet, take your time.

Once she is comfortably reaching over your hand, hold the treat far enough away that your parrot must put a foot on your hand to reach it, and tell her to "step up" or something similar, whatever you would like the cue to be. As soon as your parrot touches your hand, say "good" and hand her a treat. This is important, because you want to be sure your parrot understands what she is being rewarded for. She will quickly come to learn that "good" means "here comes a treat," and she will make note of what she did when you said

Training Talk: Punishment

Punishment is the presentation of an aversive stimulus or the removal of a positive reinforcer that serves to reduce the frequency of a behavior. Punishment can include things like flicking a bird's beak, shaking her cage, dropping her to the floor, or even blowing in her face. In other words, punishment is something that is done to a bird that she dislikes and that she will seek to avoid through other behaviors. Punishment can sometimes stop undesirable behaviors but often at the cost of a good relationship. Positive reinforcement can always be used more effectively than punishment.

it. Once again, make sure that your bird remains comfortable. If she isn't interested in a treat or being near you, try again later.

Now that your parrot is putting one foot on your hand comfortably and without hesitation, it's time to get her all the way up. Hold the treat out so that she must completely step up to get it. Give her the cue, tell her "good" when she steps all the way up, and let her take the treat. If your parrot jumps off your hand right away after getting the treat, that's okay. Remember that the more times she does something, the more confidence she'll have doing it. Be patient and let your parrot gain confidence in you and your hand as a perch. It may take some time, but it is definitely worth the effort.

Once your bird is starting to step up with confidence, try stepping her up, moving her a little, and then returning her to her perch. If your parrot doesn't step up right away at this point, leave her and come back later. Give her an

opportunity to get a treat, and if she doesn't want that opportunity, leave immediately. Your parrot will quickly learn that if she wants a treat, she needs to do what you asked right away. Soon you should have a bird who immediately steps up and is excited to do so.

Once you have trained the behavior, remember not to take it for granted. Always watch your bird and see what her body language is telling you. Is she leaning toward you, ready to be picked up? Or has she moved to the back of the cage, demonstrating disinterest? If it's not an emergency, don't make her step up if she doesn't feel like it. This way, you won't get bit and your parrot will know that you respect her. Maintaining a positive relationship with your feathered cohort should always be your number-one priority.

Training your parrot to get in and out of a carrier will save you both stress later on.

Training for the Future

With any luck, you are going to have your new feathered companion for a long time, so think forward. Make sure that your parrot is ready for and familiar with all kinds of situations.

If your new parrot is a young bird, this is especially important. Now is the time to teach her that there is little to fear.

Crate and Carrier Training

Because crate training is one of the first things you will teach your bird, there are many good reasons for making the training fun and rewarding. Your bird will need to go into the crate for trips to the vet, to accompany you on adventures, to join you when you have to move, and for safety during an emergency. It is in everybody's best interest for your parrot to think that the crate is a great place to be.

Crate training is simple but so critical that you should take plenty of time and care in the effort. You can use the method of target training (see chapter 6 for details), encouraging your parrot to follow the target into the crate in a step-by-step manner. Alternatively, you can lure her in with a tasty treat or favorite toy. Whatever method you use, make certain that your bird has seen the crate and is unafraid of it before you start working on getting her inside.

Start with the crate on the edge of a table with the door open. As your parrot sits on your hand, hold her far enough away from the crate so that she's not nervous. Offer her a treat as you bring her closer. Pay attention to her feet—if they tighten and she leans away, slow down and back up. Let her relax, and then give her treats as you move toward the crate again.

When she's comfortable being brought right up to the crate, place a treat on the lip of the threshold into the enclosure. Let your parrot reach out and pick up the treat. Put another one a little farther inside so that she has to reach farther in. Then, place a treat far enough inside that she must step in to get it. Continue this process until your parrot is comfortable walking right in and turning around to come back out. Don't shut the door of the crate until she seems completely confident being inside, and then only shut the door for a few seconds if there are several treats to eat in the back. Gradually extend how long you keep the door shut until you can leave it closed for some time.

This process can take days or weeks. Take your time. If your parrot loses interest in the treats, stop the training session. Come back later in the day and try again. If you make sure that the training sessions are

Choosing a Treat for Training

Finding a treat for training can be tricky for some parrots. Using a treat that your bird is not interested in is a waste of time. You have to utilize something that your bird really wants to eat. Observe what items your bird eats first out of her bowl. After you note her two or three favorite items, stop feeding them as part of a normal meal, and save them for use as training treats. If your training treat is something fatty, such as nuts, be sure to use it in moderation. Also, feed small pieces. Tiny slivers the size of a shelled sunflower seed can work even for training big macaws. If your parrot gets a great big treat, she made decide quickly that she's had enough.

Here is a list of some common training treats:

- Almonds
- Human-grade peanuts
- Molucca nuts
- Pine nuts
- Pistachios
- White-stripe sunflower seeds

Remember to use small pieces, not whole nuts. All nuts should be shelled before using them as training treats.

fun, you'll end up with a parrot who is racing to get into her crate. Once your parrot is trained, make sure that you periodically do crate refresher courses.

Take great care in moving the enclosure—don't swing or shake it. Make sure that your parrot gets a smooth ride so that she doesn't change her mind about the crate being a positive place to be. If you follow these training techniques, you'll always have a companion who is ready to travel.

Other Behaviors

Think about other things you might want or need to train for in the future as well. Wing clipping is a much easier endeavor if your parrot is used to you stretching and stroking her wing. My Senegal and red-bellied parrots both allow me to open their wings and patiently let me clip them. This trained behavior makes my life much easier!

This is a great time to teach your bird to enjoy a spray bottle bath as well. (Some parrots may never learn to enjoy a spray bath, though, so be gentle.) You can also try to train your bird to step up on a stick in case an unfamiliar person has to pick her up. Other potentially valuable behaviors to train may include taking liquid from a syringe in case she ever needs to be medicated and tolerating being gently toweled for visits to the vet or for grooming. Anything you can think of to train that may be relevant in the future is a valuable experience. Don't forget the most important part of training a new parrot: having fun!

Quaker parakeets are often—but not always—good at talking.

Are You Talking To Me?

One of the biggest pitfalls that companion parrot owners slip into is anthropomorphizing their birds, a fancy word meaning they imagine that their parrots have human qualities. Parrots are amazing and brilliant creatures, but they behave differently than humans. By necessity, their brains work differently. However, they speak to us in our own voices, and sometimes it's really hard not to think of them as little humans.

Communication with parrots is tricky business because they aren't little people. They deserve to be recognized for their strong intellect and amazing verbal skills but shouldn't be expected to communicate like humans. After all, parrots don't forage through the trees engaged in storytelling like two old friends catching up over a cup of coffee. Certainly they are all communicating amongst themselves, but it's often abbreviated and to the point. For example, one parrot may burst into a shriek that means "predator," and every bird will understand and take to the skies.

Because parrots are wild animals, much of their communication is grounded in survival. A call across the rainforest may bring flock members to a food source. An aggressive growl may keep breeding territory safe from invaders of the same species. Chatter and yells demonstrating well-being may attract mates. Despite parrots' obvious mastery of sound, they still aren't engaged in conversation. Parrot communication has evolved to be functional in their natural environment but not necessarily in our homes.

Parrots can understand that sounds may be attached to certain things. They are creatures of consequence. For example, when you say "bye," they may understand that you are leaving. When you say "apple," they understand that a piece of apple is forthcoming. Call the dog's name and the dog appears. These are all examples of sounds a parrot can interpret. However, when you say "be a good bird," your

Five Signs of Aggression

Aggression is displayed a little differently by individual parrots, but here are a few signs of obvious aggression.

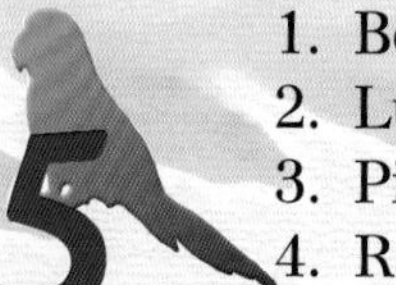

1. Bowing head
2. Lunging
3. Pinning eyes (rapidly contracting the pupil to a small point)
4. Raised neck feathers
5. Slicked-back feathers (other than neck feathers)

parrot has no idea what that means. If you say "I'll be back in five minutes," again, your parrot cannot comprehend your words. If you want to communicate effectively, you must do it on your parrot's terms.

You will know that you have crafted a rewarding relationship when your parrot understands what "scratch" means and offers her head or responds enthusiastically when you mention her favorite treat. You should have fun and label everything for your bird. Say "veggies" when you bring in breakfast, and say "water" when you change the water bowl. You can even label events. If you tell your bird "watch out" every time you pull out her food bowl as she sits on it, she'll soon know that the words mean that you're removing the food dish. What's important to remember though, is that she doesn't understand how to apply "watch out" to other situations. If someone throws a ball at your bird and you yell "watch out," she isn't going to duck unless you teach her. She only understands it as "She's pulling out my food bowl. I'd better get off it."

One of the greatest joys of owning a parrot is appreciating her ability to attach sounds to events and objects. Don't forget another form of communication that they are just as good at, though: body language. We often disregard this form of communication because humans are far less involved in the body language of feathers than birds are. Your bird watches you closely, and your actions are just as important

as your words. Think about parrots who know you're leaving the second you pick up your keys. That's body language! Think about what you are saying to your parrot with your body, and utilize that when you communicate. You don't even have to ask your parrot if she wants a scratch if she knows that the scratching motion of your index finger means the same thing. Many trainers use a variety of hand signals to communicate with and cue their parrots.

Eye pinning—rapid contraction of the pupil—is a sign of aggression in many species of parrot.

Parrots are amazing creatures and wonderful companions. Enjoying their intelligence and understanding of sound is critical to having a great relationship with them. Just don't forget that your parrot can't think like a human, but you can try to think like a bird!

Bad Behaviors, Not Bad Birds

Now that you have some training basics and ideas on how to communicate with your bird, it's time to look at a couple of problem behaviors. The best way to deal with all bad behavior is not to let it start in the first place. If you're working with a young bird, the ideal situation for molding a model parrot, you're in luck. Start addressing ways to avoid undesirable behavior now. If your parrot already has a few bad habits, don't worry. With positive reinforcement, you can train almost anything. A solution exists for just about every problem if you're willing to think it through and do the work.

Once a problem behavior has formed, it has to be solved. As a parrot lover and bird trainer, your first step in problem solving is always going to be to ask "Why?" Parrots don't engage in a behavior just for the heck of it; a behavior that's repeated is being repeated for a reason. Usually, that reason is that the behavior has been inadvertently reinforced. Keep this in mind when reading the rest of this section and when dealing with whatever undesirable behaviors your bird exhibits.

Five Ways to Encourage Good Behavior

1. Understand your bird. Learn your parrot's natural history.
2. Listen to your bird. Be observant of your parrot's behavior.
3. Interact with your bird. Teach and reward good behavior while ignoring bad behavior.
4. Respect your bird. Avoid negative reinforcement and aversive punishment.
5. Build a positive relationship. Use positive reinforcement in all interactions.

The Big Ouch!: Biting

In the wild, parrots rarely draw blood from one another. Long before aggression reaches this stage, they display many subtle warnings that violence is forthcoming. For example, parrots posture at one another, changing the way they hold their feathers, heads, and wings to convey their displeasure. I spent some long hours watching flocks of sulphur-crested cockatoos in Australia, hoping to witness aggression so that I could see what would lead one parrot to bite another. I never saw anything close. A young bird who ignores the signs of aggression may get a beak swung at her, but she probably won't have to be bitten to get the message. It's too bad humans aren't so easy.

Parrots usually bite when they want to be left alone.

At home, our parrots give us a variety of signs to let us know that we are about to get bitten. When I am occasionally bitten, I generally read the signs in retrospect, but by then it's too late. Sometimes the signs simply are not easy to read. Human body language is very different, involving lips, teeth, arms, and hands, which can make reading feathers quite a challenge—but a challenge well worth the effort.

Generally, when a bird bites, it is because she wants to be left alone, which is exactly what a biting bird gets. This is bad news for a parrot owner. Once a parrot learns that if she bites you then you will immediately leave her alone, she will be quicker to bite the next time. After all, biting seems to get the message across. Learning to read your bird, then, is the first step to preventing this behavior from occurring.

Learning to read your bird can be as simple as just noting what she looks like when she's grumpy. Do her eyes get a particular shape? Does she sit in a certain spot at the back of the cage? Does she bow her head? I know that when my grey lifts his wings, we're on good terms, and when he pulls them tight against his body, I had better leave him alone. Respecting these types of signs will go a long way toward preventing bites.

You can also teach your parrot to communicate a little better with you. If she talks, try saying the same thing every time you encounter her when she's in a cantankerous mood. Repeat the chosen word or phrase to your cranky parrot and leave. In the future, she may remember that this was the sound that you used during that particular situation. Then, when you walk up to the cage, if your parrot says "Are you grumpy?" or "Ouch!" you know it's best to leave her alone.

Biting can be situational as well. Parrots, especially Amazons, will sometimes bite just because they are excited. Other biting might involve being in a favorite place, such as a high spot or one that simulates a nesting hollow. Once again, if a bite leads to getting what a bird wants, which in this case is to stay where she is, she may bite every time she's there. Avoiding a situation is half the battle. You can also train your bird to step on a stick for situations like this and remove your flesh from the equation. Or try grabbing a favorite beak-filling treat, like an almond, to keep those mandibles busy on the way to the cage.

What? I Can't Hear You Over the Parrot: Screaming

There are several scenarios in which you may end up with a screaming Mimi for a companion parrot. Remember to start with asking the question "Why?" Why is your parrot screaming? Next, carefully observe your bird. Does she only scream when you leave the room and stop when you return? Does she stop when you yell at her to shut up? Chances are your parrot simply wants you to participate in contact calling, one of the most common reasons for screaming. Sometimes the reason is more complex, but there is always a reason. It could be to get attention, a treat, or even to persuade someone to go away. Get a notebook; write down what happened before your parrot screamed, while she screamed, and what happened afterward. You have to figure out what your parrot is getting out of screaming in order to encourage

A parrot always has a reason for screaming; the trick is to find out what it is.

her to stop the behavior or try another tactic.

Another training tool you will use frequently is to ignore undesirable behavior. This can be difficult with screaming, but if your bird engages in this behavior, don't make even a peep. The second you yell at her to be quiet, you've given her what she wants—attention. She'll continue to scream, probably at a louder volume.

Next, you want to teach her something that she can't do while screaming. For example, teach her to make a more acceptable noise. When you hear your bird whistle or call in a way that you wouldn't mind hearing all day, mark the event with the verbal cue "good," reward her, and listen for her to make the sound again. Make sure that it doesn't happen immediately after screaming, though, or you risk rewarding the scream as well. This can take some time and require ignoring an excruciating amount of screaming, but don't give up. Ignore the behavior and

Checklist for Hiring an Avian Behavior Consultant

Here is a list of qualities that a good avian behavior consultant should possess. Do not be afraid to ask as many questions as you need to find out if a consultant has these qualities.

- Ability to say "I don't know—but I can find out."
- Effective teaching and listening skills.
- Ethical professional behavior and good standing in the professional community.
- Experience with and love for parrots.
- Experience, with and adherence to positive reinforcement as the primary training tool.
- General and species-specific knowledge regarding health care, nutrition, husbandry, and behavior.
- Overall commitment to assist in creating environments in which parrots and parrot owners thrive.
- Supportive references.
- Understanding and empathy for the humans in the household, as well as the parrots.
- Willingness to treat you as a partner in the process.

reward the new call. Then, answer your bird when she calls for you with this new eardrum-friendly sound. You will have created a new, more acceptable contact call and eliminated a large amount of screaming.

If your bird isn't screaming or biting yet, wonderful! Now is a great time to get in the habit of ignoring bad behavior and rewarding good behavior. Teach your bird what sounds are acceptable now. If you catch her playing quietly, give her a treat or a little attention. Remember that every time you interact with your bird with a scratch or a treat, you're telling her that you like what she's doing—in other words, that good behavior is a way to get positive attention. Problem behaviors don't develop overnight, and it's always the human, not the parrot, who is responsible for causing them.

I Need Help!: Avian Behavior Consultants

If your parrot has a problem behavior and you're stumped, find an avian behavior consultant to work with you. The assistance of an experienced professional can be invaluable. Solving problem behaviors takes practice and sometimes a fresh eye to see what important variables you may be missing.

Before selecting a consultant, check references carefully. Talk to past clients who experienced success and others who did not succeed working with the consultant. You should be made to feel comfortable asking questions about a consultant's training philosophy without being charged. A good consultant will communicate clearly in a way that you can understand and have explanations supported by behavior science rather than solely personal anecdotes. Ask what species of parrots the behaviorist has worked with and in what capacity, as well as what parrots he or she has owned and for how long.

You may need an avian behavior consultant to solve a feather plucking problem.

Confident consultants will welcome your questions and won't require blind authority. They are open about their own limitations and will help you find the answers you need by researching issues and consulting with other professionals. Be sure that your parrot behaves comfortably with a potential consultant, as well, and that you are confident having him or her in your home. Consulting over the phone can be done but may not be as effective as the consultant directly observing as your parrot interacts in her home environment.

Chapter 6

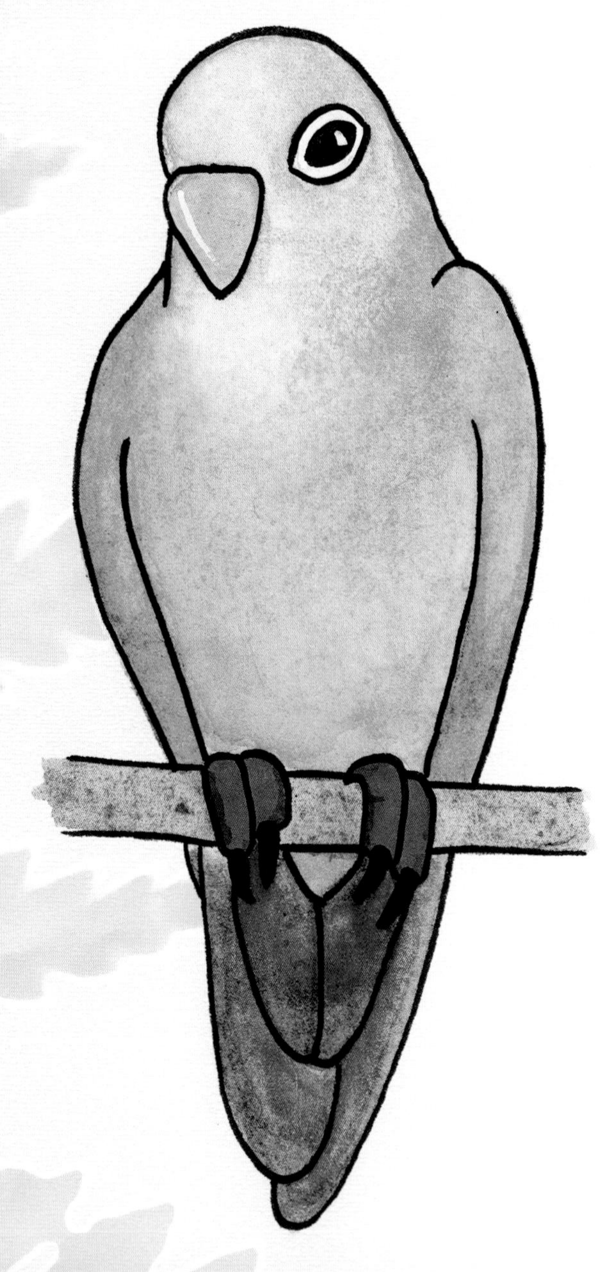

Things Are Changing!: A WELL-ADJUSTED PARROT IN A CHANGING ENVIORNMENT

A relationship with a parrot can last a lifetime, and as with any long-term relationship, there is one guarantee: Something will change. In the fast-moving and highly mobile lives that we all lead, changes in schedules, residences, and roommates are likely. However, not every pet parrot is prepared to handle a new twist to her daily routine. Sometimes these changes can cause undesirable behaviors, such as aggression, plucking, and even mutilation.

Things Are Changing!

Teach your parrot to accept changes, such as new toys, when she's young.

In the wild, a parrot's survival depends heavily on recognizing and defining every aspect of her environment, because surprises and unknowns can be deadly in a parrot's natural surroundings. A mysterious animal might be a predator, or an unfamiliar object might pose a danger. A wild parrot would quickly fly away from an unknown to keep herself safe, but a caged parrot has nowhere to go. So it should be no surprise that pet parrots often have difficulty with environmental changes. This does not mean that you should avoid changing your lifestyle; it simply means that you should do your best to prepare your parrot for inevitable changes.

Learning Young

The best way to avoid problem behaviors brought on by change is to introduce your parrot to change very early in her life. A bird in her first year is adapted to take in as much information as possible. At this age, she depends on her parents to demonstrate when something is dangerous and is more likely to be fearless. If you have a parrot this young, introduce her to as many new things as possible. You should still watch her to make sure that she is comfortable in any situation, but now is the time to let her learn that there is little in life to fear.

As you are training your fearless explorer, think about what the future might hold. There are many things that you can prepare your parrot for early in her life. Bring over new people often, and let them interact carefully with your parrot. You may have new roommates, houseguests, a new spouse, or even children down the road. Hopefully, your parrot's breeder has done a great job of early socialization, but the introduction of new things doesn't have to stop there.

If you don't have children in your house, you can invite friends with kids over so that your parrot can see that humans come in smaller and often louder packages as well. Visiting children should respect your bird by staying calm and moving slowly.

Five Things to Teach a Young Parrot

Your life with a parrot will be a lot easier if you teach her to accept change while she's young and impressionable. The following is a list of a few behaviors to teach your bird now that will help her grow up to be a happy and well-adjusted adult.

5

1. Accept spritzing for a bath
2. Allow wing and toenail trims
3. Play with new toys
4. Tolerate and not be afraid of being toweled for a medical procedure
5. Try new foods

Things Are Changing!

If you don't have kid, invite some over so your parrot can get used to them.

If you think that you might add a dog to your house at some point, have friends with well-behaved dogs bring their canine friends over. The dog and the parrot don't need to interact, but seeing that dogs are nothing to worry about at a young age can make a huge difference. Again, make sure that the dog doesn't do anything that might terrify your parrot. Even if you have a dog, a different-colored or sized dog may be considered an entirely different creature to your parrot—so don't assume she'll be comfortable with any dog. My parrots are entirely comfortable around "their" Brittany puppy but were terrified when a friend brought over his smaller, quicker Jack Russell terrier. Remember that whatever experience your bird has, she will remember it for the rest of her life, especially when she is in this learning stage. It is absolutely critical that new experiences are positive, then, if you don't want similar situations to be a problem in the future.

Another way to keep your parrot prepared for the big

changes in life is to avoid a static living situation. As mentioned previously, you can switch things up from time to time. Be mindful of your routine, and change it now and then so that your parrot doesn't get unnerved when suddenly cage cleaning happens at night instead of in the morning. That doesn't mean you should make your world chaotic—just try not to be entirely predictable. If it's possible, you might want to move your parrot's cage now and then for a change of scenery and in preparation of bigger moves. It even helps to rearrange your furniture from time to time.

If you have a parrot who wasn't introduced to new things at a young age, or if you have a parrot who, despite your best efforts, is terrified of every change, it's not the end of the world. With positive reinforcement and patience, you can convince your parrot to calmly and even happily accept almost anything. It may take longer to prep an older parrot for life changes, but the effort is worthwhile.

Variable Reinforcement

If you always reward your bird with the exact same bit of food, she eventually will decide that the reward isn't worth performing for. Variable reinforcement is a great training technique in which a parrot never quite knows what her reward is going to be. Think about it like the mailbox. If you receive catalogues that you enjoy, letters from friends, and even occasionally a check in the mail, you are more likely to run out and take a peek in your box with interest. Likewise, if a parrot occasionally gets a jackpot—a great big treat or an especially loved tidbit—when she does something right, she may be more interested in seeing what she'll get for a reward next. Vary your treats and your training will move along faster, not to mention be more fun for both you and your parrot.

Desensitization and Target Training

You can use a few tools to help your parrot deal with new and scary things. Two of the most useful are desensitization and target training.

Desensitization

One technique is desensitization. This training tool has been discussed in introducing new toys and scary items in earlier chapters. However, it is an important concept to understand. Desensitization uses small approximations (simple steps) to allow a parrot to determine that the object in question is nonthreatening. If you notice your parrot reacting to something fearfully by thrashing, trying to flee, flapping her wings, leaning away, and/or growling, then back off. Place the offending object where the parrot can see it but far enough away that she isn't reacting to it. Gradually move it closer, watching her for avoidance

Start slow with target training by just letting your parrot get used to the target.

behavior. Try interacting with the object yourself so that your parrot can see that it's nonthreatening to you. Go slow, and be thoughtful. If you were afraid of spiders, you wouldn't want someone to throw one on you, so respect your parrot's fear as well.

It is never a good idea to take the attitude of "Oh, she'll just get over it." If you force your parrot to deal with objects that she reacts to as frightening, she will get over her fear eventually, but she'll also start reacting to everything new as something that will be forced on her. For example, if you can't swim and your best friend pushes you into a pool, you may learn to swim and even get over your fear of water, but you probably aren't going to trust your best friend as much. In the same vein, being associated with negative experiences could quite easily ruin your relationship with your feathered best friend.

Target Training

Target training is another excellent way to encourage a bird to be less fearful of an object. It is also an easy, excellent method to train a large variety of behaviors, especially for a new trainer. All you need are some treats, a target, and a bird who has learned to understand an event marker, like the word "good."

You can use just about anything as a target. Just be sure that your parrot isn't afraid of it and won't destroy it if she

Click It!

Using a clicker to train is an easy way to ensure that you are marking an appropriate behavior, and clicker training has many devout followers. The event marker is communicated as a distinct and unique sound, a click, which occurs at the same time as the desired behavior. You then follow the sound with a treat. With the click, a trainer can precisely mark behavior so that the animal knows exactly what it was doing that earned the reward. You may have to juggle the treat and clicker, but a clicker can be an excellent tool. If you employ a clicker, be sure to use it consistently, and never click unless your bird performs a desired behavior. Clicking at other times will just confuse your poor parrot.

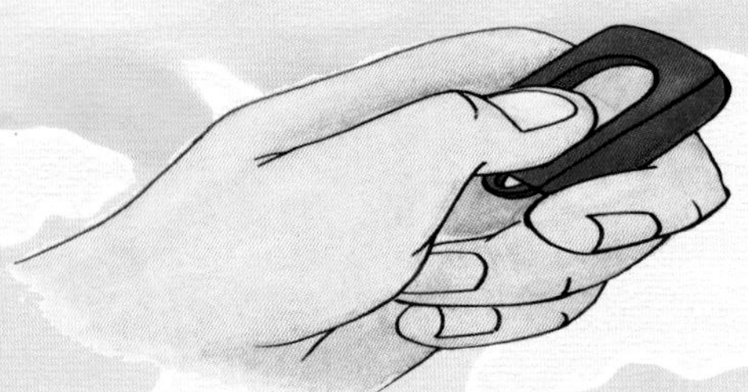

gains access to it. A spoon or a wooden drumstick are just two examples of good targets. The next step is to find a quiet place and have some fun.

Break your bird's favorite treat into small pieces that can be eaten quickly. Target training can move swiftly, and you'll want your bird to finish each reward fast. Hold the target near your parrot, and as soon as she looks at it, say "good" and reward her. Do this a couple of times until your parrot understands that the reward is for looking at the target. Then, wait until she makes a move toward the target, and reward her. Once your parrot understands that the target is the source of the reward, wait for her to touch it with her beak before you reward her. Gradually move the target away, and see if you can get your bird to follow it and touch it. With small steps, your ultimate goal will be for her to follow the target anywhere for a reward. A parrot who is target trained can make small approximations toward a scary object by moving the target toward that object, overcoming fear for the sake of a reward. They can be crate trained, trained for medical procedures, and trained just for fun. Target training is a powerful tool.

Put some toys in your parrot's carrier to keep her occupied.

Traveling

A bird who is happy to travel in a crate can journey to many great places. Some birds turn out to be wonderful travel buddies, and most can become accustomed to short trips. At the very least, you should prepare your bird to tolerate a brief drive in the car, because she will occasionally need to visit the vet or perhaps be boarded when you go on vacation. In the event of an emergency, a parrot who is used to taking short trips will be far less stressed. Regardless of where you're going, be prepared.

Although some companies make perches for cars and it's not unusual to see parrots roaming the headrest of the passenger seat, your parrot is better off in a carrier or travel cage. I've heard horrible stories of car accidents in which the driver survived but the parrot didn't. It doesn't take much of an accident to have your hollow-boned parrot flung into the windshield, an impact that's likely to severely injure her. It just isn't worth taking the risk.

Your parrot should be riding safely in a carrier or cage that's belted in. A tremendous variety of carriers and travel cages exists on the market. My favorite is just a standard kennel with a door both in the front and on the top. My birds dislike clear carriers, but they are calmer and less likely to chew on their crate if they can see out of the top and the front. For longer trips, a cage is best, but it's not as portable as a carrier. Whatever you choose, make sure that your parrot is as comfortable as possible. One warning to heed: If you can't turn off the passenger airbag, your parrot should be in the back.

Any carrier that you choose should have perching. This will be far more comfortable for your parrot than walking

Five Tips for Moving

These tips will help make moving with your parrot go as smoothly as possible.

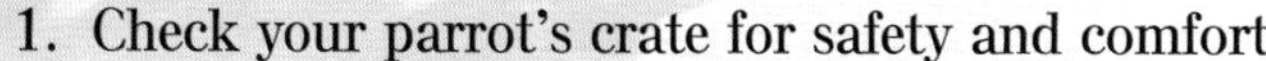

1. Check your parrot's crate for safety and comfort.
2. Find a new avian vet near your new home.
3. If driving a long distance, line up a motel in advance that takes pets.
4. Stay calm; if you are stressed and nervous, your parrot will follow your lead.
5. Take your bird for a checkup with your current vet, and obtain a copy of her medical records.

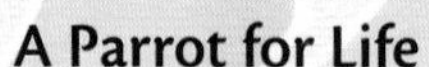

flat on the floor of the crate and sliding around. It is easy to add a perch in a standard kennel. Find a natural perch that is short enough to fit inside the carrier, parallel to the door, or cut your own. Figure out how high the perch should be so that your parrot can stand up without hitting his head and also not hit his tail. Then, drill a hole at about the middle of the crate, and secure the perch with a screw and a washer. The perch should be tight enough not to wobble so that your bird doesn't feel insecure.

When you place the carrier in your vehicle, think about your friend's comfort. She will feel most comfortable if you place the carrier so that she faces out the side windows when she sits on the perch. This way, when the vehicle starts and slows, your bird can lean into the movement of the car by shifting her weight. If she faces out the windshield, she will be flung forward and backward, making it difficult to balance. This can make your parrot carsick and generally unhappy with the ride. Also, make sure that your bird gets some air (but not a draft) and that you have a light blanket available in case you have to shade her a bit from the sun or the view.

Toys are unnecessary for a short trip, but having a few handy won't hurt. Just avoid hanging toys that might swing and hit your bird. Also, you always should travel with water for your parrot to drink. Just don't fill up the bowl more than a quarter of the way, or you'll have a sloshing mess. Slices of

Make sure your hotel allows parrots before you arrive.

watery fruit can also keep your parrot hydrated.

Just like when training your bird to get into her crate, take your time acclimating her to car rides. Glance over frequently to see if she feels nervous or sick. Start with short rides around the block, and then try longer rides. If your bird is riding happily, be sure to introduce her to windshield wipers and large trucks, both of which tend to be nerve-wracking to parrots. Even if you don't plan to take many birdie vacations, there will come a time when you're grateful that your parrot doesn't mind a car ride.

The Big Move

A parrot who will travel is a step ahead in dealing with big life changes, like moving. And chances are that if you're single with a parrot, you're going to move at some point. You may even move somewhere far. My three parrots have been moved eight times, including from California to Florida and back. We've made both the short moves across town and the sort that involve a five-day drive and nights in motels. Neither sort of move needs to be stressful—in fact, moving with parrots can be fun. Just be sure to plan ahead.

Driving

If you're making a short move with your parrot, be alert to her state of mind. The moving process can be stressful, with boxes and strange objects going by the cage. Consider putting your parrot into a quiet room where she doesn't have to witness the noise and craziness. If she's stressed out, you're going have a tough time getting her into a crate and driving her anywhere.

If you have a long-distance move, you have to think about a little more. Obtain your parrot's records from your vet for your files, and get your bird a checkup about a month before the move. You'll have peace of mind knowing that she is healthy and can handle a little extra stress. If you're crossing state lines, obtain a health certificate as close to your moving date as possible. Some states may want the certificate to allow you to cross state lines; airlines require them, so it doesn't hurt to have one anyway, just to be safe.

Five Important Things to Bring on a Road Trip

Here are five items that are essential to bring when traveling with your parrot.

1. Bottled water or water from the tap at home
2. Cooler of fruit and veggies
3. Health certificate
4. Pellets
5. Toys

For a long car ride, know ahead of time where you're staying each night. Have a driving plan with designated stops. Call ahead and make sure that your accommodations will allow for a parrot. Many motels are fine with pets but charge a deposit, and some won't be bothered with a caged parrot at all. Check to be safe. You wouldn't want to be stuck in the middle of nowhere without a place to stay for the night, and you definitely shouldn't leave your bird in the car.

Pack with your parrot's journey in mind as well as your own. Bring plenty of newspaper, paper towels, and extra dishes, and keep them someplace where you can access them easily. Pack plenty of pellets, and put fresh fruits and veggies in a cooler. Bring a bottle of water from home as well so that you don't have to worry about hotel or rest stop water. It's also a good idea to bring a spray bottle so that you can mist your bird if she looks warm (as long as she doesn't mind being spritzed).

If your parrot is a chewer and traveling in a plastic kennel, reinforce the sides of the crate. On day three of my first drive across the country, my grey had chewed a big enough hole on the side of his crate to start on the passenger seat. Some heavy zinc-free caging material attached to the inside of the crate at the vent holes will work well to allow your parrot to happily chew but not chew his way into trouble.

Flying

If you and your parrot are flying to your destination, you have even more to think about. You will definitely need your health certificate, but you also must organize with the airline in advance. Not all airlines allow birds in the cabin, and you don't want to ship your bird in the cargo hold if you can avoid it. The airlines that do take birds have a one- to two-pet limit for each flight, so you need to make arrangements for your parrots in advance if you have more than one. You also need to check specifications for travel crates. Yours will have to fit under the seat in front of you. If you're uncertain about getting an appropriate crate, you may even be able to purchase an appropriate crate directly from the airline.

Recent changes in airline security have made transporting parrots a little tricky. I had a terrible experience trying to get my grey on a plane from a bird show in Texas back to Florida mere weeks after the tragedy of 9/11. With the heightened security at the gates, the security guard

Be Careful Where You Go

If you have a parrot who travels well, you may want to take her everywhere, but be careful where you go. Avian medicine is a new science, and there are many untreatable parrot diseases. Couple this with a parrot's ability to cover sickness until it is too late, and you can see that exposing your bird to diseases is a huge risk. To minimize the risk of your bird contracting a disease, don't take her into pet stores. Parrot playgroups can be dangerous, and so can bird stores. Even if you go alone, be sure to disinfect items that have been exposed to other birds before you share them at home. If you've been playing with other birds, strip off your clothes and shower before you interact with your parrot. It's better to be safe than sorry.

Things Are Changing!

When flying, you may have to take your parrot out of her carrier to pass through security.

insisted that I remove my parrot from the crate or scan him through. Since my grey was fully flighted, I had terrible images of my poor parrot flying through the busy airport and smashing into a window, so I refused to take him out. I certainly was not going to let them expose him to X rays, either, so I refused to put the carrier through the scanner. I held up the line for quite some time until the supervisor was called and gave me permission to continue on.

Airport security has gotten a little less intense, but be prepared for extra scrutiny. You may have to remove your parrot from the crate to get her through the security checkpoint. This means that you should feel confident that your bird won't become an airport escapee. Don't let security remove your parrot from the crate themselves or run the crate through an X ray machine with your bird still in it. Be kind and patient to airport and airline staff, though. It's a privilege to be allowed to take a bird on a plane in the first place. You wouldn't want to ruin the privilege for other traveling parrot owners in the future.

Settling In

When you arrive in your new home, do the best you can to settle your best friend into her new digs. Set up her cage in the most similar situation to her old home. Then, set up her cage with the same toys and perches that she had before. She's going to have plenty of new stuff to look at, so try to keep the changes minimal until she's settled in. After a couple of trauma-free moves, your bird will take the next one in stride. In fact, the change will make her less likely to react badly to new situations.

Who's Your New Friend?

The other situational change that your parrot is likely to experience is a new human in the house. You may find that living with a roommate is financially necessary or just more fun. You may also find the significant other of your dreams or even a spouse. All of this means that at some point, your parrot is going to have to learn to live with other humans in the house.

Rules

If you and your feathered friend are going to learn to share space with another human, make sure that ground rules are

in place from the start. This is the best way to avoid conflict between species. Avoiding conflict is critical, because oftentimes it's the parrot who loses and has to find a new home. Don't bring your parrot into this situation until all humans are agreed on how the parrot fits into the household.

Parrots can become jealous of new people in your life if you aren't careful.

First, outline acceptable parrot behavior. Maybe your parrot doesn't scream incessantly, but she does call out at dawn and dusk. Some loud calls at appropriate times should be allowed in the house. Make sure that your new roommate thoroughly understands this, has heard what he or she is in for, and agrees to the terms. Maybe your parrot is allowed out of the cage on a play gym every evening when you're home. Your roommate had better agree that the avian occupant of the abode need not be permanently locked in her cage. Unsupervised roaming should not be permitted, but free time is essential. Discuss the parrot rules, and ensure that everyone has agreed to a middle ground.

Next, it is crucial that acceptable human behavior be outlined as well. Your roommate must understand the threat of household dangers to your bird. No one should feed your parrot anything that is unhealthy or toxic. No one should "punish" your parrot, even by shaking the cage or blowing on the offender. If there's screaming, the humans shouldn't scream back. (Explain that this is actually fun for the parrot!) And if your bird is an excellent talker, you might want to discuss what is appropriate to say with verve or intent around the feathered recorder.

Friend or Foe?

Now you need to figure out what sort of relationship the new roommate wants to have with the feathered one. If the new human in the equation doesn't wish to be involved, this is fine, but you may need to come up with a plan to keep him or her a noninteracting and positive influence rather than a negative influence on your bird. An out-of-the-cage parrot who is aggressive to a roommate can be a nightmare. If your roommate wants to be the parrot's friend, you'll need to come up with a different plan, but one that ensures that your parrot doesn't start hating you. Design an initial strategy for interaction between parties, but remember to be flexible. The arrangement will have to change based on your parrot's behavior.

The Big Howdy

When two animals are introduced in a zoo, it's called a "howdy." Zoos take great care when introducing two animals to one another, even if they are the same species, and zoo professionals do their best to be certain the two will get along. Howdying is basically desensitizing the animals by allowing them to gradually get used to each other from a distance. You can do the same when introducing a new pet in your household to your parrot. Allow your parrot to see the new pet confined in a crate at a distance. Gradually bring the crated pet closer until the parrot is comfortable with the new member of the household being close to her cage. Then, let the bird see the other pet wander at a distance; if it's a dog, maybe keep him on a leash. Let the new friend get closer and closer until at some point the parrot is fine with a strange-looking but obviously harmless new flock member. This is the best way to be certain that your parrot doesn't immediately associate the new pet with a negative experience.

A noninteracting positive influence in the house will respect parrot boundaries but occasionally offer treats. Teach your new roommate to read avian body language and stress how critical this can be. All it takes to make a relationship negative is for a human to continue to try to interact with a parrot who is displaying "go away" body language inside her cage. What is more irritating than a pest who won't leave you alone?

Your roommate should also learn to watch the parrot for signs of fear. Callously doing things that scare the parrot can also create aggression. If your roommate could really care less about interacting with the parrot, then he or she should just be a nonthreatening and nonannoying presence. When treats are available, though, it doesn't hurt to have the neutral party drop an occasional tidbit in your parrot's bowl. The parrot will come to understand that the other human in the house is not a bother but does occasionally add something positive to her life.

When bringing a new parrot into your home, introduce the birds carefully.

If your new roommate, or more likely, your partner, has become attached to the feathered extension of yourself, you have a little more work ahead of you. People will tell you that parrots bond with only one person, but this isn't actually true. Flocking parrots have different relationships with members of their flock other than their mate. There's no reason a parrot cannot be accepting of multiple members of a household. In all the bird shows I've worked, it's been critical that the avian performers have great relationships with many people. It is challenging to train a bird to accept numerous people, but it can definitely be done.

Follow the same plan as you would with a neutral roommate—teach the new member of the house to read parrot body language. Also, avoid negative relationships. Everyone who has gotten along fabulously with my parrots has given them space and reciprocated requests for attention. These individuals never force themselves on the birds or assume that they have an automatic relationship like the one I share after years of work and understanding. Someone who walks away when my grey puffs up but also answers my grey's whistles with a whistle back and an occasional treat is likely to become a friend.

If it seems your parrot has made up his mind that the new human is evil incarnate, don't lose hope! You have the strongest relationship with your parrot, so remove yourself from all the best moments of the parrot's day, and instead, make those tasks your roommate's job. Treats, meals, and healthy table scraps at mealtime should all be provided by the "black sheep" of the house. You should clean the cages, put the bird away, vacuum if it's a disliked activity, and be responsible for anything else the parrot doesn't enjoy. You are trying to convince the one with wings that the "new guy" is the center of everything good.

All of this will always be a balancing act. Your goal is to make sure that your parrot's opinion is that all parties are acceptable. If you're the "mate" in this equation, you may also have to make allowances during the breeding season. During this time, certain species, such as Amazons, may be intolerant of anyone but you, especially in their territory. The best you can do is not to encourage aggressive behavior. A little green beast chasing your boyfriend or girlfriend is absolutely not funny. It's humiliating to the one being chased and debilitating to everyone's relationship in the household. Also, aggressive behavior that is encouraged can escalate to a point where you have no choice but to remove the parrot from your house. Take responsibility for your parrot's actions.

A New Baby— Of the Human Kind

At some point, the new addition to your house may be a human baby. Many parrots find themselves in need of a new home when a baby comes along, so be prepared, and don't let this happen to your parrot.

I've heard many stories about parrots escalating aggressive behavior toward an infant in the household. Allowing the situation to get to the point where the baby may get bitten by the bird is dangerous, and once this happens, the parrot must go. However, parrot owners can almost always avoid these situations.

Amazon parrots may become intolerant of anyone other than their owners during breeding season.

Think about how much will change in the household and how this will affect your parrot. Try to keep her schedule normal and unchanging. This can be pretty tough with a newborn infant around, but your parrot still deserves her normal attention, time out of the cage, and playtime. If her routine and her relationship with you are the same, there will be no reason to change her behavior in an effort to get her old routine back. If this isn't something you think you can juggle, you may want to wait to get a parrot until your children are grown.

What Kind of Bird Is That?: Other Pets

A new pet may be another likely addition to your home. This can actually be easier in some ways than introducing a person. Although you can reason with a human being, you really have far more control over a puppy or a kitten, who can be locked away from your parrot. Still, it is critical that you take care in introducing new pets, be observant, keep safety in mind, and immediately teach boundaries.

If taught from a young age, almost any animal can learn to live in a cross-genera relationship. I've been a primary trainer in the introduction of a Labrador retriever pup and cheetah kitten, having watched with wonder as they sorted out their relationship as companions without any bloodshed. However, these two were equals in size and strength, which is not likely to be the case with parrots and dogs or cats. So although I believe that you can teach any young pet to respect your parrot, you still must take great care in their interactions.

Cats can be more of a danger than dogs but not necessarily on purpose. My parrots grew up with a cat who had been in the household for some time. She had little interest in them and even seemed somewhat nervous of the birds. The fact that she was frequently chased by the Senegal probably had something to do with this. Sure, it was a funny sight but very dangerous. My cat had good manners, but if she was pushed too far, one swipe of her claws could have poisoned the Senegal parrot. Cats' teeth and claws carry bacteria that are deadly to parrots if not immediately treated with antibiotics. It is not acceptable to allow your parrot to engage in aggression with another pet if you can avoid it. Never let your parrot chase your cat, no matter how funny it is. Don't encourage your cat to interact with your parrot, and never trust them alone.

It is best to not allow your parrot to interact with other pets—especially cats.

Dogs can be a less difficult addition to the home, but they should still be introduced with care. I recently added a puppy

Don't Mix & Match

Personally, I don't agree with allowing larger pets to physically interact with parrots. It only takes one misstep—a parrot who bites too hard just this once, a dog who becomes overexcited, a cat who has had enough—and your parrot can be killed. I've seen many photographs of parrots riding on dogs, but is it really worth the possibility of danger? Perhaps if we're talking about a green-winged macaw and a toy poodle, it's more of an issue for the poodle. However, if the other pets in your household can accidentally harm your parrot, it just isn't worth the risk.

to our flock, a Brittany meant to assist my falcon in the field. She is a bird dog in every sense of the word. She is trained to find birds for the falcon to hunt, protect the falcon from larger predators, and to leave the parrots alone. This all sounds like complicated training, but dogs are willing to please and are very versatile. You should be there for all initial interactions between your puppy and parrot, make sure that your parrot is comfortable, and be certain that the dog knows that the parrot is off-limits. A cue of "leave it" followed by a treat for following the request should work fine. If your dog knows to respect your parrot, and you continue to enforce the rules from the onset of the relationship, everyone will be fine. In fact, my parrots seem to enjoy watching the dog, and the grey tells her to "kennel up" frequently. The big bonus is all the pellets the dog vacuums up so that I no longer need to.

If you are not introducing a young animal that you can easily mold and handle, be careful. I have read terrible stories about dogs ripping parrots through the bars of their cages. Undoubtedly, these were canines who weren't raised with parrots. Keep in mind that all pets should be separated from your parrot, not just cats and dogs. Ferrets and large carnivorous reptiles will kill parrots if given a chance, and other small animals can bite your bird or become injured themselves. You must always be present when your mixed-genus flock interacts.

Summing Up

If you prepare your parrot for a changing world, you are far more likely to have a happy relationship for life. There is a great deal of comfort in a long-lived parrot. When you bring a dog or a cat into your home, you can almost be certain that you will outlive them. Parrots are different, and they could share decades of surprises, triumphs, and heartaches. In the next chapter, we'll look at how to keep your parrot happy in what is hopefully your ever after.

Chapter 7

Happy Parrot Ever After: CARING FOR YOUR PARROT OVER A LIFETIME

The length of a parrot's life is a hotly debated topic. The bottom line is that we're just not sure how long a parrot can live. There isn't enough research in the wild to tell how long our pets' wild counterparts might survive. We may find that parrots live far longer than we even imagined. Right now, most professionals estimate that the lifespan of larger parrot species is 50 to 60 years. This may not be the century mark that so many people ascribe to parrots, but it's still a long time. With this in mind, we should be thorough about meeting our birds' needs and doing the best we can to enjoy our lifetime with them.

Next to you, your bird's best friend is her avian veterinarian.

Is There a Doctor in the House?

Next to you, your parrot's best friend is her veterinarian. Establishing a relationship with a good avian veterinarian is a crucial part of ensuring that your feathered friend stays healthy and lives a long and happy life.

Finding a Vet

Finding an avian veterinarian is something that you should do before you even bring your parrot home. A good vet is a friend for your parrot's lifetime and should be visited annually. Also, if you are planning to move, you should immediately seek a vet in your new town. Keeping a good avian vet's number on the refrigerator will be an important part of your parrot's long and happy life.

Many websites can assist you in finding a local vet. Check the "find an avian vet" websites and see who pops up. Also, check with www.aav.org, the website of the Association of Avian Veterinarians. You should also check with the American Board of Veterinary Practitioners (ABVP) for veterinarians certified in Avian Practice. These vets have received further education to become specialists in avian medicine. Go to www.abvp.com and search under "find a diplomate" for vets in your area. Your best bet is ABVP, but the truth is that it can be difficult to find a good avian vet, so look everywhere. If you can't find a listing, call a few local cat and dog vets and see if they know anyone who treats birds as well.

Once you have at least one name and phone number, check up on your prospects. See what sort of experience they have, even beyond their practice. Do they own a pet bird or breed parrots? How long have they been in practice treating parrots? It is also appropriate to ask for references. Normally, you would just ask your new neighbors about their veterinarian, but your neighbors may not have birds. Just because it isn't as easy to find folks who require their services doesn't mean that you shouldn't get to chat with clients.

When you first meet your avian vet, be a little critical. Scrutinizing different clues will tell you whether you're employing an able vet. Bedside manner is wonderful if you can get it, but it's not crucial. A better start is to look at the clinic's surroundings. Is it clean, and does it smell nice? Are there bird-related items in the reception area and tools for avian care in the exam rooms? Ask for a tour; you're entitled.

Ask questions of the staff to see if they are knowledgeable about parrots. I fired a vet who treated my birds when I lived in California seven years before because the receptionist looked at the hooded peregrine on my glove, flipped through my file, and asked if that was my Senegal. Even the staff should at least know the difference between a parrot and a raptor. If not, the vet obviously isn't seeing many birds and getting much practice. You should also be able to have a conversation with your vet that proves that he or she is familiar with current avian medicine. I wouldn't suggest quizzing potential vets, but a conversation about recent treatments and their thoughts on keeping a parrot healthy should be enough to give you an idea of their expertise. You must trust your vet. Second-guessing him or her in a medical emergency can be stressful for you and dangerous for your bird. Find a vet in whom you have confidence before you have to bring a sick parrot to the office. You can develop that confidence by bringing your bird in for routine examinations.

An examination of your bird should be thorough, thoughtful, and compassionate. Your vet should ask you

Five Signs of a Good Vet

If your avian vet possesses all the following qualities, you've probably found a keeper!

1. Clean hospital
2. Courteous, well-trained staff
3. Excellent cageside manners
4. Great references
5. Knowledgeable in recent bird information

myriad questions about your bird, including queries about diet, housing, behavior, and history. A good vet with a well-trained tech will take your bird out of the carrier quickly and in as stress-free a manner as possible. They will perform a careful physical examination, inspecting your bird's entire body. They will draw blood to do diagnostic tests. They will also take a throat swab, as well as a fresh fecal sample from the carrier. This should all be done quickly and with attention to your parrot's level of stress. If your annual examination goes well and the office follows up quickly with results and a willingness to answer questions, chances are that you have a great vet. Take your parrot in once a year and watch for any signs that you should take her sooner.

Have a plan for paying emergency vet bills so you can avoid overextending your finances.

It's Not Cheep!: Paying the Vet Bills

You'll learn quickly that avian care costs more than caring for a dog or cat. The vet isn't robbing you—it's just that avian care requires different instruments, more testing, and extra expertise. After all, there's only one species of dog and one species of cat, but there are hundreds of species of parrots. Each parrot species has different blood chemistry and is prone to different problems. It's a big job to be a bird vet.

A standard avian checkup will cost roughly twice the amount that it would for a dog or cat, and in some places more. If your bird is actually sick, you can expect to pay far

Microchipping

A microchip is a tiny computer chip about the size of a grain of rice used to uniquely identify a parrot. It is inserted into the breast muscle of a bird with a hypodermic needle. A scanner can read the chip, and the number displayed is kept in a database, enabling the bird to be traced back to her owner. The insertion can be a little bit uncomfortable, but it heals rapidly and never bothers the parrot again. Microchips are used for identifying dogs and cats as well, and zoos frequently use chips to distinguish individual animals during their annual exams. The cost of the chip is sometimes included in "new parrot" exam packages at vet offices. Most animal shelters and veterinary offices have scanners for reading microchips on hand. Microchipping is the best way to prove ownership, and it can help your bird find her way home to you if she were to fly away or be stolen.

more. Additional tests will be required, and if surgeries and overnight stays are necessary, the bills can really mount. A parrot owner needs to be aware of this and be prepared in the event of an emergency. You have to know how you'll pay your bills and perhaps even be aware of where the cutoff is or if there will never be a cutoff. The price of veterinary care will not get less expensive, either—the costs continue to rise.

Develop a plan for parrot health-care costs. Will your vet take a payment plan? Many will but only for a certain amount. You should discuss this with your vet so that you can plan ahead. Do you have a savings account? Could you spare it all for a broken wing, a cracked beak, or a debilitating disease that could cost thousands of dollars? Do you have enough on your credit cards to cover an emergency? And if you do, how long would it take to pay them off? These are a few ways to cover expenses in a pinch.

Recently, the possibility of pet insurance for birds has become a more viable one. A variety of plans is available, but only Veterinary Pet Insurance (VPI) seems to include parrots and not focus mainly on cats and dogs. This company offers an avian and exotic plan with charges based on the species of parrot that you're insuring. VPI charges a monthly premium and gives you the option of going to whatever vet you wish. You pay up front, and they reimburse you based on a very specific schedule. An annual checkup just about pays for the cost of a year's worth of insurance. Pet insurance is worth considering if a small chunk of change every month is easier for you than trying to pay for an emergency. Every year more pet insurance options become available, so continue to educate yourself, and look into all possibilities. Keeping abreast of the changes in pet insurance is the only way to choose what's best for you.

The other option is to set aside money every month in an account that's meant for parrot emergencies. Hats off to you folks who are capable of such savings. It's probably the smartest way to prepare for unexpected illnesses. If you're like me, though, you may not have the willpower unless a bill comes in the mail every month. Whatever makes sense to you is the best plan for your parrot—just make sure there's a plan.

How to Spot a Sick Parrot

Your vet should be the first line of defense with any big behavior problem or change. If your parrot starts plucking or

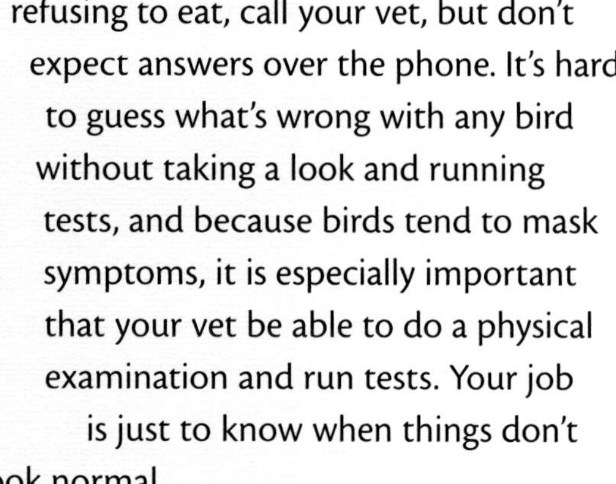

Ruffled feathers, lethargy, and drooping eyelids are all signs of a sick bird.

refusing to eat, call your vet, but don't expect answers over the phone. It's hard to guess what's wrong with any bird without taking a look and running tests, and because birds tend to mask symptoms, it is especially important that your vet be able to do a physical examination and run tests. Your job is just to know when things don't look normal.

The most obvious signs of illness in a sick bird are a fluffed-up appearance, drooping wings, and half-closed eyes. If your bird looks like this when she should be active and lively, get her to the vet right away. You should also notice if your bird is regurgitating (other than to feed you—in this case, the sign of a happy, bonded parrot) and has loose stools. Droppings that are runny, mixed together, or contain blood, mucus, or undigested food are a sign of sickness. Other more subtle signs of sickness include changes in posture, damaged feathers, difficulty breathing, and irritated eyes. It is best to learn what your bird looks like and how she acts when she feels good. It's also a good idea to weigh your parrot and be familiar with her normal weight on a gram scale. Once she has finished weaning and growing, a big weight fluctuation may be an indicator of illness. Any change in your bird's routine, such as not spending time out of her cage or being less vocal, can be the sign of a problem. If you watch for even subtle signs, you'll know when to get your bird to the vet for an examination.

There are a couple things that will trick the new parrot owner, however. It is much better to be safe than sorry, but don't let these common changes fool you. The first is that parrots do not cough and sneeze like humans. If you get a nasty cold, your parrot may learn a great imitation of it, but she's not sick. Parrots with a cold may wheeze and have liquid running from their nostrils, but they sound nothing like a person sneezing. Also, as you watch your bird's droppings for changes, be aware that food colors change the appearance of parrot poop. Don't have a heart attack the first time you give your bird beets. Her poop will be deep red. Droppings will also change hue depending on the pellet color of choice for the day. Look in the bowl and see what

Five Tips for a Healthy Parrot

5

1. Teach your parrot to sit on a scale calmly, and weigh her monthly. You'll be able to note sudden drops in weight, which should cue you to visit your vet promptly.
2. Feed a healthy, varied diet.
3. Observe your parrot every day for signs of illness.
4. Keep cages, perches, toys, and play gyms clean.
4. Have an avian veterinarian examine your parrot annually.

colors are left. If your bird's droppings look awfully blue, chances are that's the only color pellet missing in the bowl.

Other Caregivers: Parrot Sitters

Vets may not be the only caregiver on whom you spend your hard-earned cash. More than likely, there will come a time when you need to travel somewhere without your parrot. In this instance, you need to find someone knowledgeable and comfortable with parrots.

Some vets do board parrots, but ask yourself if you really want your bird in a building where other sick parrots come in for treatment. Avian illnesses tend to be airborne, and some are highly contagious. Even if healthy parrots are kept separate from sick clients, there's still a risk. Your vet may be wonderful, but you could be putting your parrot in danger.

Some pet stores, bird farms, and dog kennels also board parrots. Again, this is a risk that you may not wish to take. A sick dog or cat is easy to spot, but a sick parrot is not. Unless all parrots coming in have had recent and extensive health checks, including blood work, your parrot could be at risk of contracting an illness. Some places only take one or two parrots at a time, and if the birds have a health certificate, your parrot will be less likely to be exposed to disease. If boarding is your only option, be sure to discuss with the facility owners or

It is usually best to hire a sitter instead of boarding your bird when you go away.

staff what their policies are for avoiding transmission of illness, as well as what general care will be provided.

Oftentimes, the best option for a caretaker while you're on vacation is a pet sitter who will come into your home to feed and spend time with your parrot. If you choose to go with a professional pet-sitting service, ask around. See if you can find other parrot owners who have used that service, and if you cannot, ask the service for references. Also, check to make sure that the business is properly licensed and insured. Then, find out what the establishment's policies are, especially concerning the prevention of disease transmission. If your caretaker is looking after multiple households with birds, you'll want to be sure that he or she takes every precaution.

If you have a neighbor, friend, or relative who's confident with parrots and happy to look after your feathered child, then you're in luck. Your parrot will be less stressed if a familiar person is caring for her in her own home. Just make sure that the number for the vet is on the refrigerator, along with a way to contact you. Then, be sure to write up a note with any pertinent information and set it next to the emergency kit.

Preparing for the Worst

No matter where you live, there is always the possibility of some sort of disaster. I've had to prep for hurricanes,

What's in Your Emergency Kit?

Here's a list of items that are essential to have in your birdie emergency kit. Almost all of them can be purchased at a pharmacy or supermarket. Remember to check expiration dates periodically, and replace expired products as needed.

- Antibacterial hand gel
- Antibiotic ointment
- Bandage scissors
- Cornstarch
- Gauze
- Hemostats
- Oral syringe
- Pedialite or Gatorade
- Povidone-iodine solution
- Tweezers
- Vet wrap

earthquakes, flooding, and fires. Nowhere is entirely safe, but if you're prepared, you'll have peace of mind that your parrot will remain secure.

Have an exit plan for a disaster. First and most importantly, keep a crate ready to transport your parrot. If you have more than one parrot, have enough crates for everyone. Don't keep the crate locked away in a closet somewhere, either. It should be easily accessible, lined with newspaper, clean, and ready to go. If the roof has fallen or you've been given minutes to evacuate, every second counts. You must have a plan for how you're going to load up your parrot and get her out of the house.

Hopefully, if you have to immediately evacuate, you'll be in a position to get whatever else you need to care for your parrot elsewhere. You should also have a plan for what to do if the world outside has gone nuts and you can't go anywhere. Your house could be structurally sound, but you may not have running water or electricity. Keep enough pellets on hand for at least a week at all times, maybe some canned vegetables or other canned goods to supplement your parrot's diet, and plenty of bottled water. Stock up on all the standards for yourself in an emergency, but make sure that there's plenty for your parrot as well. You'll also want to set up an emergency kit specifically for your bird.

A sturdy fishing tackle box is a great place to store everything you'll need for a parrot emergency. Fill the box with items to clean and dress wounds, like povidone iodine or another antiseptic, gauze, antibiotic ointment, vet wrap, and bandage scissors. You'll want tweezers and hemostats in case you need to remove a feather or something stuck in the skin, as well as cornstarch to staunch bleeding. Pedialite or Gatorade and a syringe are critical for handfeeding liquids to birds who are in shock or who are dehydrated. A small bottle of antibacterial hand gel is a great addition as well. Pack the box thoughtfully, and be sure to change out things with expiration dates from time to time. Hopefully, you will never need a plan or an emergency kit, but if you ever do, you'll glad that you have them.

Having a fully stocked bird first aid kit in an easily accessed place is essential.

When You're Gone

One last sad but important thought before we move on to some fun stuff is that you must have a plan for your parrot outliving you. More than any other pet—except maybe tortoises—parrots have the potential to outlast us. You wouldn't want your parrot to have an uncertain future if something happened to you, so plan now.

First, find godparronts. The idea is worth giggling over, but have a serious conversation with friends and family. With whom would your parrot live? Make sure that the home you've decided on knows that you're serious and is truly willing to take on your companion. Then, put that person's name in your will or living trust.

Even if you get a parrot when you are young, she may still outlive you. Plan accordingly.

If you are single and living alone, you also have to have a plan for how your parrot will be taken care of if you suddenly become sick or have an accident. How will someone get in the house, and who will know how to manage your feathered friend? When I had my appendix taken out a couple of years ago, I had a surprise stay in the hospital. Fortunately, there was a spare key to my apartment in my desk drawer at work, and since work was a literal zoo, there were several able-bodied friends to look after my mighty flock of three. Make a plan yourself, and you'll have one less thing to fret over if you unexpectedly can't make it home.

One last thing to consider when owing a parrot who might outlive you is manners. Seriously, if your parrot cusses up a blue streak, she may have a harder time finding a new home. What if she constantly screams? Making an effort to raise and keep a well-adjusted parrot will give her a better chance for a new life. Sure, your parrot will miss you, but she will also move on, just like in the wild were she to lose a mate. Give your bird the best possible chance for a future with or without you.

Losing a Parrot

Even the very best parrot caretakers lose beloved parrots to unforeseen tragedies, illnesses, and

Training for Medical and Grooming Procedures

As long as you're training your parrot, you may as well train with some medical and grooming procedures in mind. Today, with the use of positive reinforcement, the possibilities are limitless. I've seen video of trainers who have taught a parrot to calmly accept blood draws without restraint in return for a treat. While I'm not suggesting that you attempt this particular procedure, how about training your bird to accept a toenail clipping? Go slowly, using your chosen event marker when your parrot allows you to get the clippers close to her feet, and then reward her. Gradually get closer while being mindful of her attitude. Eventually, try slipping the tip of a toe in the clippers; when your parrot allows this, use your event marker and reward her. Do this until she will let you set any toenail in the clippers. Finally, take the tiniest bit of the tip of a nail off, and give your parrot a huge reward. Work on this behavior often until she happily lets you trim her toenails. If training this is a possibility, think of all the wonderful things you might teach your parrot to do!

age. It's hard to even think about, and I hope it never happens to you. If you do lose your friend, allow yourself to grieve as deeply and long as you need. She wasn't "just a pet," and don't let anyone try to convince you of that. Think about how to honor your lost friend and whether burial in the yard, cremation, or burial at a pet cemetery is right for you. There is no wrong decision, only the one that will give you the most closure.

Life of the Party: Training for Fun

Parrots can be trained to do many fun tricks.

Training your parrot is the best way to build a positive relationship while also having a tremendous amount of fun. Now that you've trained a few important behaviors, such as going into a crate and stepping up on your hand, you can use the tools you've learned to train some fun stuff, too. Remember that positive training is fun for your parrot and stimulates her brain. If you have an extremely intelligent parrot (and you undoubtedly do), there's no reason you can't try a few fun behaviors and entertain your party guests.

Speak to Me

If you have a talking or mimicking parrot, then getting words, phrases, and sounds on cue is a blast. The great thing is that once a parrot figures out the training process of "capturing" a verbal behavior, each new word will become easier to get on cue. Capturing is simply rewarding a behavior that your parrot does and training her to perform that behavior on cue, rather than teaching her a new behavior.

Being creative with your cues is fun as well. Choose cues that can be easily slipped into a sentence, making it appear like your parrot knows exactly what she's saying. Whatever you choose to train, have fun. This is the greatest part of having a parrot—the relationship!

The best time to start training your parrot is during a period when you will be home for most of the day. This way, your bird will have a large chunk of time to figure out what you are asking of her. Then, you just have to listen. If she is more likely to chatter when you're not in the room with her, you might try occupying yourself in another room, listening closely. As soon as you hear your bird say the chosen word, call out "good!" and walk into the room to reward her. ("Good" is the event marker; you could also use another word or clicker, as long as you are consistent.)

After you have done this for a while, your parrot is going to figure out that saying that word not only gets her a treat, but it gets her attention, too. Soon, she will offer it frequently. Now it is time to teach her the cue. Maybe you want to get the ringing of the phone on cue, and your cue is going to be the word "phone." To teach this, start to say the cue to your bird. When you say "phone" and your bird says nothing, then she gets nothing. If she offers the ringing sound when you didn't ask for it, then she doesn't get anything, either. It's hard, especially when your bird is confused and you feel sorry for her, but be patient. She'll figure it out. Eventually, she will offer the sound right after you have said the cue. When this happens, reward her big, and watch the wheels turn in her head. It shouldn't take long from here; just keep saying the cue and waiting for the sound. In no time at all, when you say the cue, your bird will give you the behavior. Now that your bird understands the training routine, you can get other words on cue more easily. Expect some confusion at first about there being more than one treatworthy sound, but be patient and you'll soon have your bird gabbing up a storm.

Wave Goodbye

Training your parrot to perform physical behaviors on cue can be easy as well. The wave is perhaps one of the most simple, especially for a bird who readily steps up. To teach this behavior, hold a hand or finger in front of your bird as if you want her to step up, and say "wave." As soon as her foot starts to lift, say "good," and give her a reward. Gradually move your hand away each time you ask for a wave until your parrot understands that the cue is the word, not the hand. You can shrink the cue to just a little finger wiggle if you would like to use both a hand signal and a verbal cue. Once your parrot understands that you are asking her to lift her foot, you can start to shape the behavior into a wave. Ask for a wave, but don't use your event marker until the behavior is a little more pronounced every time. If your bird is interested in the training session and the treats, she'll offer bigger waves, wanting to figure out what gets a treat. Soon, your parrot will be waving hello and goodbye on cue.

Waving goodbye is one of the easier tricks to teach

Conclusion
SOME FINAL WORDS

They say that an animal trainer's pets are generally the worst trained. I find that that's not true at all. It isn't that we have anything to prove, it's just that training parrots is so much fun! Training is the highest level of interaction you can have with a parrot. She's listening and watching you, and you are listening and watching her, both of you trying to figure out the other. There is no greater feeling than when a parrot's eyes light up because she just figured out what you've been trying to ask her to do. No doubt the same light is in your own eyes. Don't ever stop training or learning, and I can promise you a wonderful lifetime with your parrot, whatever changes your life brings.

Resources

Organizations

American Federation of Aviculture
P.O.Box 7312
N. Kansas City, MO 64116
Telephone: (816) 421-3214
Fax: (816)421-3214
E-mail: afaoffice@aol.com
http:// www.afabirds.org
The American Federation of Aviculture is a nonprofit national organization whose purpose is to represent all aspects of aviculture and to educate the public about keeping and breeding birds in captivity.

Avicultural Society of America
PO Box 5516
Riverside, CA 92517-5516
Telephone: (951) 780-4102
Fax: (951) 789-9366
E-mail: info@asabirds.org
http:// www.asabirds.org
The objectives of the Society are the study of foreign and native birds; the dissemination among the members of information for the care, breeding, and feeding of birds in captivity; the perpetuation of species that are threatened with extinction; and the publication of matter pertaining to aviculture.

Aviculture Society of the United Kingdom
Arcadia-The Mounts-East Allington-Totnes
Devon TQ9 7QJ
United Kingdom
E-mail: admin@avisoc.co.uk
http:////www.avisoc.co.uk/

The Gabriel Foundation
1025 Acoma Street
Denver, CO 80204
Telephone: (970) 963-2620
Fax: (970) 963-2218
E-mail:
gabriel@thegabrielfoundation.org
http://
www.thegabrielfoundation.org
The Gabriel Foundation is a nonprofit organization serving parrots, by promotoing education, conservation, rescue, rehabilitation, adoption, and sanctuary.

International Association of Avian Trainers and Educators
350 St. Andrews Fairway
Memphis, TN 38111
Telephone: (901) 685-9122
Fax: (901) 685-7233
E-mail: secretary@iaate.org
http:// www.iaate.org
The International Association of Avian Trainers and Educators was founded to foster communication, professionalism, and cooperation among those individuals who serve Avian Science through training, public display, research, husbandry, conservation, and education.

The Parrot Society of Australia
P.O. Box 75
Salisbury, Queensland 4107
Australia
E-mail:
petbird@parrotsociety.org.au
http: //www.partosociety.org.au

Emergency Resources and Rescue Organizations

ASPCA Animal Poison Control Center
Telephone: (888) 426-4435
E-mail: napcc@aspca.org (for non-emergency, general information only)
http:////www.apcc.aspca.org

Bird Hotline
P.O. Box 1411
Sedona, AZ 86339-1411
E-mail:
birdhotline@birdhotline.com
http:////www.birdhotline.com/

Bird Placement Program
P.O. Box 347392
Parma, OH 44134
Telephone: (330) 722-1627
E-mail: birdrescue5@hotmail.com
www.birdrescue.com

Parrot Rehabilitation Society
P.O. Box 620213
San Diego, CA 92102
Telephone: (619) 224-6712
E-mail: prsorg@yahoo.com
www.parrotsociety.org

Veterinary Resources

Association of Avian Veterinarians
P.O.Box 811720
Boca Raton, FL 33481-1720
Telephone: (561) 393-8901
Fax: (561) 393-8902
E-mail: AAVCTRLOFC@aol.com
www.aav.org

Resources

The Association of Avian Veterinarians works to share information among avian veterinarians, educating both professionals and pet owners about the best practices of avian care.

Internet Resources

The Animal Behavior Management Alliance
www.theabma.org
The Animal Behavior Management Alliance, (ABMA) is a not-for-profit corporation with a membership comprised of animal care professionals and other individuals interested in enhancing animal care through training and enrichment.

BirdCLICK
www.geocities.com/Heartland/Acres/9154/
A site and e-mail list devoted to clicker training pet birds.

Behavior Works
www.Behaviorworks.org
This is the site of Susan Friedman, Ph.D. It provides information on the online class "Living and Learning With Parrots" and a link to the writings of Dr. Friedman.

Exotic Pet Vet.Net
www.exoticpetvet.net
Exotic Pet Vet.net is a site designed by exotic veterinarians. The site offers many articles about avian diseases and care.

HolisticBird.org
www.holisticbird.org
Holistic Bird has a large variety of articles on behavior, nutrition, and diseases. The site's focus is on keeping parrots healthy through addressing every aspect of a bird's well being.

The Parrot Pages
www.parrotpages.com
The Parrot Pages believes that the best pet bird owner is an informed owner. The website provides information and a home for avian products, breeders, clubs, and organizations in the form of a multitude of links.

Yahoo Groups
www.yahoo.com/groups
Be sure to peruse Yahoo Groups for your species of parrot or particular needs. There is likely a group that at this very moment is discussing your parrot question. The Internet has become a fabulous resource of opinions, but don't forget that they are just that, opinions! Not everything said and posted on the internet is true. That said, this is a fantastic place to do your parrot homework.

Conservation Organizations

Loro Parque Foundation
www.loroparque-fundacion.org
This Spanish organization works to preserve parrots and their habitats through education, research, and responsible breeding programs.

Kakapo Recovery Programme
www.kakaporecovery.org.nz
An organization devoted to ensuring the survival of one of the world's most endangered parrots.

World Parrot Trust (UK)
Glarmor House
Hayle, Cornwall TR27 4HB
Telephone: 444 01736 751 026
Fax: 44 01736 751 028
E-mail: uk@worldparrottrust.org
www.worldparrottrust.org

World Parrot Trust (USA)
P.O.Box 353
Stillwater, MN 55082
Telephone: (651) 275-1877
Fax: (651)275-1891
E-mail: usa@worldparrottrus.org
www.worldparrotrust.org
The World Parrot Trust works toward the survival of parrot species in the wild and the welfare of captive birds everywhere.

For Further Reading

Books

Brinker, Bobbi. *For the Love of Greys*. Lancaster, OH: Lucky Press, LLC, 2005.

Deutsch, Robin, *The Healthy Bird Cookbook*. Neptune City, NJ: T.F.H. Publications, 2004.

Forshaw, Joseph. *Parrots of the World*. Neptune City, NJ: T.F.H. Publications, 1978.

Gallerstein, Gary A., *The Complete Pet Bird Owner's Handbook*. Minneapolis, MN: Avian Publications, 2003.

Harrison's Bird Foods, *"Advances in Companion Bird Nutrition*: Proceedings of the 2004 Avian Nutrition Seminar," March 2004.

Heidenreich, Barbara. *The Parrot Problem Solver*. Neptune City, NJ: T.F.H. Publications, 2005.

———. *Good Bird: The Guide to Solving Behavioral Problems in Companion Parrots!,* Minneapolis, MN: Avian Publications, 2004.

Sparks, John and Tony Soper. *Parrots: A Natural History*, New York: Facts on File, 1990.

Articles

Friedman, S.G., "The ABC's of Behavior," *Original Flying Machine*, November/December 2000.

—-, "The Help at Hand," *PsittiScene*, May 2002.

—-"He Said, She Said, Science Says," *Good Bird Magazine*, Spring 2005.

Friedman, S.G. and Bobbi Brinker, "Early Socialization: A Biological Need and the Key to Companionability," *Original Flying Machine*, September/October 2000.

——- "The Nature of Greys," *Bird Talk*, November 1999.

Gilardi, James D. and Charles A. Munn, "Patterns of Activity, Flocking and Habitat Use in Parrots of the Peruvian Amazon," *The Condor*, 1998.

Hess, L. et al., "Estimated Nutrient Content of Diets Commonly Fed to Pet Birds," *Veterinary Record*, March 2002.

Levey, Douglas J, and Carlos Martinez Del Rio, "Perspectives in Ornithology, It Takes Guts (and more) to Eat Fruit: Lessons from Avian Nutritional Ecology," *The Auk*, October 2001.

Iwaniuk, Andrew N. and John E. Nelson, "Developmental Differences are Correlated with Relative Brain Size in Birds: A Comparative Analysis," *Canadian Journal of Zoology*, December 2003.

Pepperberg, Irene Maxine. *The Alex Studies: Cognitive and Communicative Abilities of Grey Parrots*, Cambridge, Massachusetts: Harvard University Press, 2000.

Pepperberg, Irene M. and Spencer K. Lynn, "Possible Levels of Animal Consciousness with Reference to Grey Parrots (*Psittacus erithacus*)," *American Zoology*, 2000.

Sol, Daniel et al, "Big Brains, Enhanced Cognition, and Response of Birds to Novel Environments," *PNAS*, April 2005.

Wright, Timothy F. and Gerald S. Wilkinson, "Population Genetic Structure and Vocal Dialects in an Amazon Parrot," *Proceedings of the Royal Society of London, Biological Sciences*, March 2001.

Articles by the Author

"Are You Talkin' to Me?," *Bird Times*, August 2005.

"The Basics of Dealing with Bad Behavior," *Bird Times*, February 2004.

"Entertaining a Bird Brain," *Bird Times*, December 2004.

"Fun With Food," *Bird Times*, June 2005.

"Get It on Cue," *Bird Times*, August 2004.

"Get the Bite Out," *Bird Times*, October 2004.

"Healesville, Australia- Aussie Parrot Paradise," *Good Bird Magazine*, Spring 2005.

"It's a Jungle Out There—and in Here, Too!," *Bird Times*, February 2005.

"Parrot Training for the New Owner: Grooming Your Parrot into the Perfect Companion," *Good Bird Magazine*, Summer 2005.

"Stepping Up," *Bird Times*, April 2005.

"Rescue Me," *Bird Times*, October 2005.

"Who's Your New Friend? Introducing New Members of the Family," *Good Bird Magazine*, Winter 2005.

Magazines

Bird Talk
3 Burroughs
Irvine, CA 92618
Telephone: 949-855-8822
Fax: (949) 855-3045
http://www.birdtalkmagazine.com

Bird Times
7-L Dundas Circle
Greensboro, NC 27407
Telephone: (336) 292-4247
Fax: (336) 292-4272
E-mail: info@petpublishing.com
http://www.birdtimes.com

Good Bird
PO Box 684394
Austin, TX 78768
Telephone: 512-423-7734
Fax: (512) 236-0531
E-mail: info@goodbirdinc.com
www.goodbirdinc.com

Parrots Magazine
Imax Ltd.
Riverside Business Centre
Brighton Road, Shore-by-Sea,
BN43 6RE
Telephone: 01273 464 777
E-Mail: info@imaxweb.co.uk
www.parrotmag.com

Index

Boldface numbers indicate an illustration.

Index

Index